CHARLY

Deseret Book Company
Salt Lake City, Utah
1980

CHARLY

JACK WEYLAND

Library of Congress Cataloging-in-Publication Data

Weyland, Jack, 1940–
    Charly.

    1. Title.
PZ4.W53735Ch [PS3573.E99]   813'.54   80-11216
ISBN 0-87747-814-7 (hardbound edition)
ISBN 0-87579-121-2 (paperbound edition)

Printed in the United States of America
  10   9   8   7   6   5   4   3   2   1

Chapter One

"*Charly?*" the funeral director asked.

"Yes, Charly," I answered. "Her given name was Charlene but she hated it."

The funeral director paused respectfully, cleared his throat, and politely objected, "Generally we put the given name on the headstone."

"Then this will be an exception for you, won't it?" I replied.

* * * * *

It all began six years ago, between my junior and senior years at Brigham Young University. I stayed at home that summer and worked as a computer programmer for an engineering consultant firm in Salt Lake City.

Dad and I had jogged two miles that early June morning and were eating our nutlike cereal on the patio overlooking the city.

"Sam, you remember the new manager I was telling you about," Dad asked as he downed his vitamin pill, "the one that was transferred from New York? Well, he's finally found a house and his family moved out here last week. He's got a daughter your age. Naturally she doesn't know anyone in Utah." He paused, hoping I'd volunteer and not force him to spell it out.

"That's too bad," was the best I could do.

"I was wondering if you'd take her out once just as a favor."

1

"I'm kind of low on money right now. I'm saving to get my jeep fixed—I can't get it out of four-wheel drive."

"Maybe I could help you out," Dad said.

"Is this girl LDS?" I asked.

"Well, no."

"Sorry—I only date LDS girls." I was enjoying this. It was the same discussion we'd had in high school, but this time the roles were reversed.

"I'm not asking you to marry her," Dad pleaded. "Think of it as missionary work."

"All right," I reluctantly conceded, "I'll take her to the Visitor's Center and then buy her a milk shake."

"Can't you do any better than that? She's the daughter of our regional manager. Why don't you take her to the country club for dinner? I'll treat."

"In my jeep?" I pressed.

"No, take my car."

"Good idea, Dad," I said, basking in my brilliant victory.

The elation was short-lived, however, as the event arranged by the two fathers approached. Somewhere in this city, I thought, a few days before the date, is a girl who was born and raised near New York City, who now is attending Columbia University, majoring, of all things, in philosophy, and I'm going to be stuck with her for one long, dreadful evening. I made a half-hearted attempt to read about the life and works of Immanuel Kant, hoping to use the material as a life raft in a dying conversation.

A few days later, I drove to her house, a cross between a fort and a colonial mansion, designed as nearly as I could tell after the Alamo.

"Sit down," her father said, ushering me into the living room, which was big enough to house two racquetball courts. "Charlene will be here in a minute. Can I get you anything?"

"No thanks," I said, feeling a drop of nervous perspiration cascade down my right arm. "Hot out, isn't it?"

"If you think this is bad, you should be in Manhattan in the summer."

A long pause followed while I fantasized about being on the Provo River casting into my favorite fishing hole—or anywhere except here trying to think of something to say to my dad's boss before taking his philosophical daughter out.

"It's the humidity," I finally said.

"Really?" her father answered, getting up, no doubt deciding that if this conversation were to last much longer he needed a drink.

"Sure," I said.

Just then Charlene's mother entered the room.

"This is my wife."

"It's a pleasure to meet you," I beamed, standing up in an imitation of Cary Grant from an old movie.

We all sat down.

"Sam was just telling me about humidity."

"Really?" his wife said from behind her perpetual society smile.

"Yes," I said. "Have you noticed the difference in humidity between here and New York?"

At that moment Charlene sauntered in. I was impressed. She looked like a model for a diet soft drink. I stood up with an extended hand.

"And this is our daughter Charlene," her father beamed.

"Charlene, it's a pleasure to meet you."

"The pleasure is mine, I'm sure," she said, looking strangely at my outstretched hand. As we shook hands she, still smiling sweetly, dug her fingernails into my palm.

"Would you like some sunflower seeds?" she asked, heading for a bowl she had placed on the mantel of the fireplace.

"Sam was just explaining about humidity," her father commented as he got up again to finish mixing a stiff drink to help him through this.

"It must've been fascinating," she said dully, thrusting the bowl of sunflower seeds at me. "Go on, take a big handful."

Believing it to be some obscure East coast tradition, I grabbed a bunch of seeds. "There's a difference in humidity between here and New York."

"So what?" she asked.

Nervously I cracked a seed between my teeth and picked out the meat with my tongue. I should have wondered why nobody else was having any, but it wasn't until months later I discovered this was Charly's way of protesting being forced to go out with a hayseed from Utah.

"I believe I'll have a drink too, dear," her mother said.

"What?" I asked.

"So what if there is a difference in humidity?" she pressed.

"That's why you feel so uncomfortable now," I answered, then finished off several seeds quickly in succession.

"I don't feel uncomfortable," she said.

I looked around for a bowl to put the shells in, didn't see one, and therefore suavely stored them in my left hand, saving my right hand free in case there was a need to shake hands with anyone else.

"That's because we're inside. Wait until later and you'll feel uncomfortable."

"You mean when I'm alone with you," she countered.

"That's not what I meant."

By this time I had a pile of saliva-covered shells in my left hand. Her parents stared hypnotically at the shells, waiting to see what I'd do with them. I suppose they thought this to be some obscure western tradition.

I hadn't read that many etiquette books, but somehow I suspected it wasn't proper to plop the mess on their marble coffee table.

There was only one thing to do. I popped the shells in my mouth and chewed them up and swallowed.

"All right!" Charlene beamed.

"Well, you kids run along and have a good time," her father said, standing up quickly to get rid of us.

We drove silently for several blocks.

"How much is your dad paying you for taking me out?" she finally asked.

"I was happy to take you out," I lied.

"I bet. What would you think about turning off the air conditioner? It's freezing in here."

"No, it's not. Besides, I very seldom get to drive a car with air conditioning. Why don't you check the blower so it's not aimed directly at you?"

She sat and glared at the dashboard, rubbing her arms for warmth.

"Tell me, Charlene, how do you find the difference in elevation between here and New York?"

She looked at me as if I were crazy.

"See, we're higher here," I babbled away, "and that means the air is thinner, so you have to breathe faster than you did in New York. Have you noticed yourself breathing faster here in Utah?"

She glared icily at me, enjoying my suffering. Finally, after what seemed a year, she said, "Don't call me Charlene."

"What, then?"

"Charly."

Unable to let disaster alone, I plunged on. "See, if you climbed some of these mountains, you'd find yourself getting tired because the higher you go, the less oxygen there is, and the less oxygen there is, the faster you have to breathe. That's what I meant about fast breathing."

She shook her head and mumbled, "How could my own father do this to me?"

I decided to abandon the weather and play my trump card. "What do you think about Immanuel Kant, seventeen twenty-four to eighteen o four?"

She opened the side window and deliberately adjusted it so the hot outside air was blowing directly on me.

"It's a waste of gas to have the air conditioning on and the window open."

"You never told me how much your dad is paying you to take me out."

"Not enough," I said, giving up.

She folded her arms and turned away. When I looked at her a few minutes later, there were tears on her face.

"I didn't mean that—I'm sorry. Look, I'm turning off the air conditioning. Oh, and there's a Kleenex in the jockey box."

"And why would I want one?" she challenged.

"Because you're crying."

"I'm not crying. My contacts are bothering me."

"Probably a result of the difference in humidity between here and New York! Anyway the Kleenex is still in the jockey box."

"I got my own," she muttered, rummaging through an old leather bag. Eventually she found one crumpled, previously used tissue, which she smoothed out and used.

"Will you take me home, please?"

Whirling into a shopping center parking lot, I made a U-turn and hurried back toward her house. We drove in silence.

I shut off the motor at her curb. "I'm sorry things didn't work out."

"It's no big thing."

"No, it's probably my fault. To tell you the truth, I wasn't looking forward to this. I figured you'd be rich, spoiled, and boring."

"And?"

"You're not boring."

"I'd better go in now," she said, reaching over to open the door. "It's getting late."

"It's only seven o'clock."

"Well, I have a big day tomorrow. I have to wash my tennis shoes."

We started for her porch.

"Look, you think it's easy going out with a girl from New York? My dad and I thought you'd like the country club—especially my dad. I never would've taken you there myself. It's very expensive."

"Listening to you talk about humidity and watching old golfers slap each other on the back? No thanks."

"Believe me, it's not my idea of fun either," I said.

"No?"

"No."

We stood at her door, staring at each other.

"What is your idea of fun?" she asked.

We stood and talked about things we had always wanted to do but never could find anyone to do them with. A few minutes later we drove to a park and blew all my dad's money on a roll of tickets to the Ferris wheel.

"What's your name?" Charly asked the tall, white-haired attendant as he helped us into the Ferris wheel car.

"Raferty."

"Mr. Raferty, I'd like you to meet my fiancé. He's just proposed and you're the first one we've told."

"She's just kidding," I explained. "Actually, we've just met."

Apparently Mr. Raferty was hard of hearing me. "Congratulations, kids."

"Why, thank you," she smiled. "Sam and I want to ride your Ferris wheel for a long, long time. You understand, don't you?"

"Sure, I'm not that old," he said with a wink.

We rode and talked. Up over the trees, the laughing

children, the crying children, the picnicking families, the merry-go-round, and then back to earth and Mr. Raferty, who gave us a smile as often as he could.

"Are you a Mormon, Sam?"

"Yes, why?"

"Well, is there some way I could learn about Mormons this summer while I'm here?"

"I think I could arrange that," I said.

*　*　*　*　*

The missionary discussion, held a week later, had gone well, I thought. The missionaries had left after the cake and ice cream. Charly and I walked in the backyard looking at the garden.

"Well, what do you think about what we talked about tonight?"

"What are those?" she asked.

"Cabbages."

We walked between the rows of the garden. I don't think she had ever seen such a large family plot.

"Hello, cabbages."

She always kept a few vegetables ahead of me.

"Charly, what about the discussion?"

"What do you do with all this stuff?"

"We can it."

"Doesn't my dad pay your father enough?"

"What about the discussion?"

"I don't believe a word of it. And these?"

"Garden beans. Why don't you believe it?"

"The whole thing is ridiculous. Prophets, angels, apostles, books of gold. The hardest thing to understand is why you believe it. I mean, you look like an intelligent person."

"Is that right?"

"Of course, looks can be deceiving."

We'd come to the raspberries. I picked a few for us. "You know, it'd help if you were a little more humble. That's the trouble with you Easterners—you all think you know everything."

"Columbia's taught me to use logic and reason. You should try it sometime." She popped a handful of raspberries in her mouth. "These'd be terrific with ice cream."

7

"There's nothing wrong with logic and reason, but to know for sure if this is true, you also need to pray about it."

"I know what this is—corn. Right?"

She knelt down and touched a little corn plant. "Pray to what?"

"God."

"I haven't made up my mind yet about Him or Her or It."

"It's a Him."

"Why does it have to be a Him?"

"I don't know why. It just is."

"You're sure?"

"Positive."

"How come you're all so positive about this? It just drives me up the wall. Where in Utah can I find some old-fashioned doubt and uncertainty?"

"I know that Joseph Smith was a prophet, and that the Savior has restored his church back on earth."

"You can't know that for sure."

"I know it."

"You believe it, but you can't know it. There's nothing in this world you can really know."

"If you pray about this and continue to study, God will manifest to you that it's true. And then you'll know."

She patted the top of another corn plant. "Did you know the Indians called this maize?"

"Look, we can pray again about this if you want. I know a place behind the lilacs where it's secluded." I pulled her to the little "lilac room" where I had played fort as a boy. I remembered it as a big room, but that had been when I was eight years old. It had shrunk since then.

"It may be a little crowded," I confessed as we looked at the one-foot opening through the bush.

"Are you kidding? I'm not going in there."

"All right, let's try behind that peach tree." I dragged her to another spot, but just as we got there, our neighbor started his lawn mower a few feet beyond us on his side of the fence, giving us both the idea that this wasn't going to work out. Secluded spots are hard to come by these days.

"Do you want to say the prayer?" I yelled above the roar of the lawn mower.

"Not on your life!" she yelled back.

I knelt down. "Kneel down, okay?"

Just then the mower stopped, which was even worse, as I imagined our neighbor peering through the fence at us.

"If this ruins my nylons, you're in big trouble," she warned as she knelt down.

"Now fold your arms and close your eyes and I'll say the prayer."

After four words I could tell she was getting up again. I opened my eyes and looked up. She was just standing there, looking at me strangely.

"Sam, you're definitely crazy," she calmly said before turning to walk to the house.

On her way, she grabbed a handful of raspberries.

" 'By their fruits ye shall know them!' " I called to her.

Chapter Two

A week later I took Charly fishing at Strawberry Reservoir. We left at four A.M. When we arrived, I rented a boat, rowed to my favorite spot, threw out both anchors, and started to fish.

She curled up in an old army blanket and went to sleep.

By the time she woke up, I had caught four nice trout, the sun had come and driven off the patches of fog from the lake, and ten other boats had joined us.

She studied the people in the boats near us, who were all quietly watching their lines.

Suddenly she stood up, cleared her throat, and with a Kissinger-like accent addressed the other boaters: "I suppose you know why we've asked you all here this morning. If it meets with your approval, we'll dispense with the minutes and proceed."

The boaters glanced at her with disbelief.

"Because some of you have been putting marshmallows on your hooks, the Utah Fish and Game Department, hereafter referred to as the UFGD, has asked me to speak today. Clinical reports just released indicate that the fish in this lake have fifty-three percent more cavities."

She paused and then yelled sharply, "DO YOU KNOW WHAT THIS MEANS?"

She waited for an answer but nobody spoke. Most tried to ignore her, but that was hard to do.

"It means the UFGD must now stand the expense of sending a trout through dental school!"

"Charly?" I said.

"Yes, Utah," she answered demurely.

"Normally we don't talk between boats."

"So?"

"So sit down and be quiet."

She sat down. I baited her hook and threw it out. In a few minutes, her line began to feed out smoothly and steadily. When she set the hook, I could tell it was going to be big. Screaming and giggling, doing an impersonation of Captain Ahab after Moby Dick, she reeled in the line and soon I dipped the net into the water and brought up a four-pound trout.

After I had taken care of the fish, she stood up again. "Do you want to know how I caught this fish? I used peanut butter on the hook. It sticks well, and it does not—does not, I repeat—cause little fish cavities."

Quickly I pulled in both anchors and began to row away.

"We recommend creamy instead of chunky!" she yelled as her parting shot.

"Sam, where are we going?"

"Away."

"Is the fishing better where we're going?"

"No."

"Oh, I embarrassed you, is that it? Go ahead and say it."

"You embarrassed me."

"You've got no sense of fun, do you? Life is for laughing."

"I laugh."

"No, you smile faintly."

To prove her wrong, I laughed. Even to me, it sounded weird.

"No good. Too forced. It's not spontaneous."

"I laugh responsibly."

"And could you define that for us, Senator?"

"After the work is done, if there's time left over, then I laugh and have fun."

"You've got it all backwards. You're supposed to laugh during the work. That's one of the things that's wrong with you. You never do anything spontaneous. All the time in your head little gears whirl."

She dipped a cup into the lake and threw the water at me.

I continued to row, my head dripping water.

"No, Sam, you're supposed to stop rowing and throw some water on me. It's what we call a water fight. Can you say that for me, dear? *Wa-ter fight.* It's one of those happy, spontaneous things people do in this dull world."

I continued to row silently.

"Sam, does someone plug you in at night to charge up your battery pack? Did the water damage your memory bank? Sam, speak to me so I'll know you're human!"

"The water here is deep. If the boat were to capsize, it'd be dangerous." I headed the boat toward the dock.

"Why should the boat capsize?" she asked apprehensively.

I kept on rowing.

At the dock, I unloaded the fishing gear and my shoes before heading out a little way from the shore. Then I took my string and measured the depth.

"Why did you put those things on the dock and then come out here?" she asked.

I sat down beside her in the boat.

"The water here is only five feet deep."

"I guess I shouldn't have dumped water on you. Right?"

"So I'm not spontaneous enough, is that it?"

"Oh, it's really nothing," she said meekly.

With a sudden lunge, I pushed her into the lake.

"You dirty rat!" she yelled after she came up again.

"I'm laughing now, Charly. Do you hear me?"

"You . . . you computer!"

"That's the nicest thing anyone has ever said to me."

When I tried to help her into the boat, she rocked it sharply, throwing me also into the water.

* * * * *

"How much more time are you going to be spending with Charly?" my father asked one morning at breakfast.

"I don't know. Why?"

"Her father called me into his office yesterday and made it perfectly clear that they don't want her to become a Mormon."

"Not much chance of that."

"Then why is she still taking the discussions?"

"It's a hobby with her—tripping up the missionaries."

"Well, her parents are still worried," he said, reshuffling his newspaper for emphasis. "And there's another thing."

12

"What's that?"

"Your mother and I are worried you might be getting interested in her. She's not a member of the Church, and you know how we feel about the importance of temple marriage."

"I feel the same way, Dad."

"Good, then quit seeing her. You've done enough fellowshipping."

"No."

"Why not?"

"She's my friend."

"There are plenty of good LDS girls in our ward without you chasing her."

"I'm not chasing her. It's just that she loves to go fishing." I realized that wasn't quite accurate.

"All right, then limit your activities to fishing."

"Fine," I agreed nonchalantly as if she didn't mean anything to me, but at the same time wondering why I hadn't dated anyone else since I'd met Charly.

That's why the only activities we shared for the next few weeks were listening to the missionary lessons and going fishing.

Three weeks later we were back on Strawberry Reservoir in a boat. Fishing was slow that day.

"You haven't said much about the Church since I tried to pray with you."

"I decided to be fair. We Easterners are noted for our fairness."

"Yes, I've heard about the Salem witch trials," I countered.

"Not bad, Sam. Stick with me and I'll make you a wit. You're halfway there now." She opened a sack of oranges, tossed one to me, and kept one for herself.

For a few minutes she concentrated on peeling her orange. Then, quietly and soberly, she said, "I've read the Book of Mormon."

"You have?" I said, completely shocked, since around the missionaries she never answered a question seriously. "What do you think about it?"

"You're not going to make us kneel in prayer in this boat, are you?" she gently teased.

"No, just tell me how you feel about the Book of Mormon."

13

For a long, serious time, she studied the ripples in the water. And then she began. "Humor 'em along, I said. Take the lessons, go to church, and then when summer's over, leave 'em laughing. After all, it's just a part of the Utah tour.

"I grew up in New York. As a child my parents made sure I was exposed to culture and reason—the Museum of Natural History, the Hayden Planetarium, the Metropolitan Museum of Art. I know opera arias the way you know cowboy songs." She paused. "Do you know what I'm saying?"

"No, what are you saying?"

"I'm an intellectual! I'm not one of your sweet farm girls—there's nothing sweet about me. And then you come to me with your 'two-and-a-half-minute talks.' Why not three minutes, for crying out loud! Sam, I was all set up to spend the rest of my life laughing at the world. There was so much to ridicule, so many balloons to pop. It'd take a lifetime."

"Don't give me a dissertation, Charly. What about the Book of Mormon?"

That's when the tears began to flow.

"What's wrong?"

"It's true. Of all the rotten luck, it's true."

"What is?" I asked.

"The whole thing—the plates, the angels, all of it." She continued to cry.

"You mean you believe it?"

"Sure, don't you?"

I ate my orange and wondered what I was supposed to say.

"Then why are you crying?"

"Don't you see? When fall comes and I go back to school and my friends come up and ask, 'Did the Mormons get you?' what do I say?"

"Bear your testimony."

"They'll think I'm a fool."

"What are you interested in? Truth or pretense?"

"You're asking me that? That's the same question I've been using as a weapon against the world up to now. Don't you see? I've been hoisted up on my own petard."

"That can be painful," I replied, touching my kneecap. "I hurt my petard once playing baseball."

"Sam, Sam, Sam," she said, tears still streaming down

her face, but a slight smile creeping out, "what have we done to each other?"

* * * * *

To say that the announcement of her impending baptism brought everlasting joy and happiness would be wrong. Her parents were furious, and since my dad worked for her father, my parents were unhappy too.

The best way to describe my parents is to say that they are the kind of people you find giving workshops at stake leadership meetings. Polished, poised, and perfect. My father doesn't even get messy when he works on the stake welfare farm.

"You're tearing their family apart," he accused me one evening.

"Dad, it was entirely her decision—I didn't talk her into it. She wants to get baptized."

"Well, her parents aren't going to allow it."

"She's over eighteen."

"Are you suggesting she disobey her parents?" my mother asked.

"The Church is true, isn't it?" That stopped Mom for a while—but not Dad.

"Her father thinks, and I tend to agree, that she should give this some time. Maybe a year or two. That way she can make sure it's what she really wants. She's very unstable sometimes. Her father told me that last year she refused to eat grapes from California."

"Maybe," my mother joined the fight, "you could encourage her to wait a year before she joins the Church. And then I don't think you should see her for a while."

"Why shouldn't I see her?" I asked.

"Because she's not a member of the Church," she replied.

I tried to explain to Mom that what she was suggesting was the Mormon equivalent of Catch-22, but since she hadn't read that book, I didn't get very far.

I could have argued much more successfully with my parents than I did. In high school, I was a pro at Disagreement. But after two years of being on a mission, and receiving little homey letters from my mother and dictated business letters from my father (he even sent me copies of talks he gave as a high councilor), I'd lost my enjoyment of making them squirm. Besides, after hearing my mother that night in family prayer plead for blessings for me, I decided to at least approach Charly.

"Are you getting baptized just because of me?" I asked her on the phone.

"You mean because of your personal charm and magnetism?" she teased.

"Something like that."

"My parents have, of course, brought that up, so I've thought about it. You're not too bad-looking, you know. Maybe I'm doing it just to please you. It does please you, doesn't it?"

"Only if it's because you believe it."

"Maybe it is just because of your charisma—except for one thing."

"What's that?"

"It's hard to see how your charisma could reach out into my room while I read the Book of Mormon. Sam, when I read that book, I have a feeling, I don't know how to describe it to you, but I feel that it's true. You want to know something else? I'm praying now, and you know what? Someone's listening."

*   *   *   *   *

When I went the next Saturday to pick her up for afternoon stream fishing, we were confronted by her parents.

"I think it's ridiculous for my daughter to think about becoming a Mormon, don't you?" her father opened.

"No, not really."

"Dad, please, we've already gone through this before."

"How could you let yourself be brainwashed into something like this? You know they'll make you pay ten percent of your income, don't you?"

"I don't have an income, but when I do, I'll pay tithing because I want to, not because anyone's forcing me."

"What have you done to my daughter?" her father demanded.

He got me in the middle of my lemonade. The question

16

started me choking. Finally, with red face, I gasped, "I haven't done anything."

"He's right," Charly smiled. "All we do is go fishing."

"Look, Charlene has a history of becoming fascinated with things and then losing interest. I'm sure the Mormon church doesn't want unstable converts, does it?"

"Unstable?" Charly cried out. "Is that what you think I am?"

"What about the harp lessons? You begged us to buy you a harp, you took lessons for six months, and then absolutely refused to touch it again. Are those the workings of a stable person?"

"Daddy, that was in junior high school!"

"Charly, if I may say something," her mother interrupted, "the Mormons are always saying on TV that the family is important. If that's true, and if you believe in the Mormon teachings, then you should show it by helping our family stay united and strong."

"How do I do that?" she asked.

"By not joining the Mormon church."

Another Catch-22. The discussion ebbed and flowed while I quietly watched, nursing a lemonade made out of real lemons. This was better than a TV soap opera.

An hour later, Charly obtained reluctant permission to be baptized. I'm sure her father figured the whole thing would blow over in a while—just like the harp lessons.

I baptized her the following Saturday. She was beautiful in white. When I dream about her now, I visualize her in white.

Her parents didn't come.

Chapter Three

"Nice going, corn plants."

Charly and I sat, both wearing jeans, barefoot in the middle of my parents' garden. We had been weeding but were taking a rest, facing away from each other, my back propped against hers, with our bare feet planted in the warm, dark soil. The cornstalks towered over our heads and we heard the hum of bees, while overhead small, puffy clouds paraded by. I liked the lusty smell from the nearby tomato plants and the feel of her warm back against mine and the combined smells of her perspiration and shampoo.

"Nice going, Earth. Nice going, Father in heaven," she purred.

She moved around and sat in front of me.

"Sam, I've never felt so clean in my life."

"Oh, yeah?" I smiled. "Well, your feet are dirty."

"Sure, but that will wash off. I meant a different kind of clean. Is it true that when I was baptized all my past sins were washed away and I started off with a clean slate?"

"That's right."

"Do you believe it?"

"Sure. I taught it for two years on my mission."

"So, right now, I'm as pure and clean as any other girl in the ward?"

"Except for your feet, sure. Why do you ask?"

"I just wanted to be sure I understood. And Heavenly Father will forget any bad I did before my baptism?"

"He'll forget the things we repent of."

"Isn't that terrific?" she beamed. "What a nice thing to do for us."

"I agree."

"But what about you? What about your sins? It's been a long time since you were baptized."

"I have to keep repenting. That's one of the reasons we take the sacrament each Sunday: so we can renew the covenants of baptism."

She asked me about my mission and I told her my stock of faith-promoting stories. After that, she asked me to tell her about the temple and especially about temple marriage. I told her as much as we used to tell people on my mission.

"Sam, will I always feel as good about the Church as I do now?"

"I don't know. I hope so." I paused and then continued. "There's one thing you have to remember. The Church is perfect, but the people in it aren't."

"Is that important to remember?"

"I'm afraid it is."

* * * * *

With a jeep and not much sense, you can drive up a mountain to a place overlooking all of Salt Lake City. I took Charly there one night and after parking, we got out and stood side by side looking down at the city. I put my arm around her.

"I see what you mean about the altitude," she said.

"What?"

"You know—you talked about it on our first date—about the altitude making a person breathe faster."

I leaned over and kissed her for the first time. It was very nice, and I was about to repeat the process when she suddenly touched her eye.

"Oh, no! My contact fell out!"

Going to the jeep, I turned on the headlights and gingerly proceeded again to where she was standing. I knelt down and moved my head from side to side looking for the reflection of the light from the lens. Finally I found it and gave it to her.

Back in the jeep a few minutes later, after she had cleaned the lens and placed it in her eye, I started to lean over the gearshift lever when she touched my lips with her finger and warned, "Let's not push our luck. I don't have insurance."

"Insurance?" I asked.

"For my contact lens."

* * * * *

"Are you going to ask me to marry you, Sam?" she asked one Saturday at the country club pool while rubbing suntan lotion on my shoulders.

"You're not supposed to ask that."

"Male chauvinist. Why can't I ask it? Are you?"

"I don't know for sure."

"You men are so impetuous."

I ignored her and lay back down on the warm sun deck. A few minutes later I heard a faint voice disturbing my sleep. "Are you awake? You're getting a sunburn."

"I'm awake," I answered sluggishly.

"Sam, I've thought it over. I accept. You're a lucky man."

I sat up. She leaned toward me as if she was going to kiss me, but instead she slapped me on the shoulders. "Race you to the diving board."

She beat me there and we took turns diving; she was a hard act to follow. Once while we waited our turn, she punched me in the chin in slow motion and teased, "Sam, you son of a gun, asking me to marry you when we've known each other only a few weeks. You've got some nerve, kid."

She did a perfect swan dive and I followed with the same boring dive I'd been doing since the eighth grade.

"Why the joke about marriage?" I asked the next time we stood in line.

"Who said I was joking?"

Again she stood at the board. Turning back, she addressed the swimmers who were waiting in line to dive. "For the next dive, I must have silence so I may concentrate," she announced dramatically, with a slight European accent. "This dive has passed from generation to generation in my family. If you will be quiet, then I will do it for you today."

20

A hush fell over the swimmers. She surveyed the pool area. A waiter carrying food to a lounging couple stopped to wait for her.

"So . . . I will do it."

Slowly approaching the middle of the board, she stopped, put her arms out, apparently reaching for psychological strength. Then, summoning courage, she raced to the edge of the board, jumped high into the air, tucked her knees gracefully, yelled "Geronimo!" and did . . . a cannonball.

* * * * *

To tell the truth, I wasn't sure when she was serious and when she was kidding. For one reason, she switched from one to the other so fast I couldn't follow her.

I wasn't sure why she was joking about marriage until the first week in August when I took her to the computer facility where I had been working that summer.

"You know all about this?"

We sat in front of the computer console on a Saturday night when nobody else was around.

"Sure, want to learn?" I helped her push the right buttons. In a few minutes, page after page of results tumbled out.

"You seem to fit in this room so well,"she said, her voice strangely tense. "It's all so antiseptic and devoid of feeling. Tell me, do you ever sweat?"

"Not in this room. They have to keep it at a constant temperature."

"I mean any place."

"Sure, why?"

"Just wondering. You analyze everything, don't you —just like a computer."

"Charly, what's wrong?"

"I picture you plotting graphs after each date."

"What are you talking about?"

"Okay, I'll tell you. You never tell me how you feel about me. If you can't put it in words, could you give it to me in numbers?"

I studied her for a long time, completely bewildered,

and then finally confessed, "What do you want me to say?"

"Oh, forget it!" she snapped.

"I like you very much. Is that what you want me to say?"

"I'm sorry I brought it up."

"I don't see why you're so upset, Charly."

"Okay, I'll tell you. I love you—I mean really love you."

"Oh," I said lamely.

"I'm not sure why. Part of it has to do with your being responsible for my being baptized. You'll always be special to me for that. And then you're so unlike any other guy I've ever known. I can't sort it out in my mind, but I know I love you—but you seem so content to just continue where we are right now."

"Oh," I said.

"Sam, I'm sorry for throwing my feelings at you. It'll probably turn you off and you'll get scared. Right?"

"No, of course not," I said, suddenly turned off and scared.

"How do you feel about me—marriage-wise?"

I panicked. It was the same feeling I'd had after being on my mission for twenty-two months and receiving letters from the girl who had waited for me. In one letter she sent me a list of all the kitchen appliances she had accumulated for us during the two years. She had not only the usual sheets and towels and chinaware that prospective brides squirrel away, but also a microwave oven, and a deep freeze, and a vacuum cleaner. She was sending me, three months before my release, samples of wedding announcements for me to choose from. She was asking me to pick names for our children—eight names.

After that, I knew panic.

Fortunately, she later saved me a lot of trouble by marrying the salesman who had sold her a deep-fat fryer.

But now again, with Charly, the panic was back.

"Well?" she asked.

Nervously I cleared my throat. "There's nobody in the world I'd rather be with right now than you. We've really had a lot of fun together, haven't we?" I chuckled, hoping to ease the tension.

"What about marriage?"

"Marriage," I repeated, "marriage in the temple is one of the most important things we can do in this life."

"What about marriage to me?" she pressed.

This was a side to her I had never seen before. Instead of the light-hearted banter usually characterizing our dates, I was facing a tense, emotional girl who, as near as I could tell, had just proposed to me.

"I'd have to think about it—but, look, if I were to draw up a list, you'd certainly be right up there near the top."

"What's wrong with me?"

"Nothing. I just haven't thought much about it. You see, all my life when I've pictured getting married, it's always been in my mind that it'd be someone from Utah or Idaho or even California—someone who's been raised in the Church. You know, there's an advantage to the children if both sets of grandparents are LDS."

She stood up and ran away.

I followed after her down the empty hall.

"Charly!" I called as loud as I could.

She stopped and looked back. Then I stopped.

"I think I'm falling in love with you, but could you give me a little time?"

"Is there anything that Utah Mormon girls do that I should learn—you know, like drying apricot pits?"

"I don't think so."

"If you want me to, I'll learn to make plastic grapes in Relief Society."

On the way out to the car, I kissed her. My lips had no problem appreciating her; it was my mind that was fighting the idea of marriage. I kept picturing her parents lifting my future children on a bar stool and offering them a scotch and soda.

Chapter Four

Near the end of August, we were walking around a department store on a Saturday afternoon. We had just passed the maternity clothes.

"How many children do you want, Sam?" she asked, modeling one of the dresses from the rack.

"At least six."

"So many? How come? Religious reasons?"

"That's right."

"Six kids. Nearly a baseball team."

"They come one at a time. That way you can make all your mistakes on the first one."

"Easy, fella, I was the first one."

A while later we walked by the toy department and a row of dolls. She picked up six, but one fell down. "I can't get six, Sam," she said, putting down all the dolls except one. "I'll be a good mother, Sam. As good as if I'd grown up in Utah."

We got what we needed, but on the way out I remembered I had meant to buy a coupling for our water hose. Since she was not really interested, we agreed to separate and meet later. She coyly suggested the jewelry counter.

I found the hardware section and the coupling quickly but then ran into a former missionary companion and his wife and baby. We talked for ten minutes. When I finally arrived at the jewelry counter, Charly wasn't there. After waiting for a while, I started to walk around to see if I could find her.

After walking aimlessly around the store for a few minutes, I heard a strangely familiar voice over the P.A. system. "Sam, Sammy, do you hear me? This is Mommy. The nice men in the store let me talk to you on their big radio. Sammy, wherever you are in the store, stop and listen to Mommy."

I stopped and looked around to see if anyone was looking at me.

"Sammy, darling, if you can hear me, listen carefully. Remember when Mommy bought you a big bag of popcorn last week? Sam, go to the popcorn machine and Mommy will be there. Do you understand? The popcorn place. Mommy has a big bag of popcorn for you. Mommy loves you, dear."

A man standing next to me grabbed a handkerchief and blew his nose. "Poor little guy," he muttered to himself.

I stormed over to the popcorn machine. There was Charly with a bag of popcorn in her hand and a record she had bought.

"I got a Passion for you," she smiled, referring to the record.

I grabbed her arm and escorted her out of the store.

"Sam, do you like Bach?" she asked. I kept marching. "You're mad at me, aren't you."

"Did you find your boy?" a security guard asked as we breezed by.

"Big for his age, isn't he?"

"Get in," I ordered when we reached the jeep.

"Yes, sir!" she teased.

I climbed in and glared at her as she nonchalantly munched her popcorn. "Why don't you grow up? You think the world is made for your amusement?"

"Is that a rhetorical question, or do you want an answer?"

"What if there'd been an emergency? You just think you can tie up their P.A. system for your own amusement?"

" 'Attention, shoppers,' " she mimicked, " 'there's a blue-light special this hour on shredded muslin at two dollars a yard.' You call that an emergency?"

"There is such a thing as responsibility," I shot back.

"I'm sure there is, and there's also such a thing as being a stuffed shirt."

I drove like a madman. Screeching to a stop in front of her house, I turned to her and unleashed my big attack. "You talk about marriage. Well, I'm not ready to get married to someone who hasn't grown up yet."

"Why do you have to be such a self-righteous bore?" She jumped out, started up the steps, stopped, paused, and then rushed back to me. "Sam, I really should apologize."

"Okay."

"I didn't offer you any popcorn, did I?"

And that was when she dumped the entire contents of the bag over my head and stormed into her house.

* * * * *

I suppose I planned to let her stew for a couple of days before calling to tell her she was forgiven. But when I finally called on Tuesday, her mother told me Charly had decided to go back to New York early for school. She didn't want me to write or call or ever see her again.

For a solid week, I tried to reach her. When I finally obtained her phone number and called, she hung up on me. About a month later, the dozen letters I had written showed up in a large envelope—unopened.

In the meantime I had gone back to BYU.

There are ten thousand eligible girls at BYU. To get over my grief, I decided to date as many as possible. With good time management, and taking advantage of all the free activities, I set a goal to take out a dozen different girls each week.

At first it was fun. It's like being an alcoholic locked in a wine cellar—one hardly knows where to begin. Do you concentrate on blondes for a month and then move on? Or do you focus on California girls first and then move eastward?

One thing I learned to avoid was dating too many girls from my own ward. It starts talk when girls realize you've taken four of them from their dorm to the same campus movie on one weekend.

The point with high-volume dating is—don't get involved. To the freshman girls, you talk about how soon you want to get married. To the senior girls, you tell them you are thinking about changing your major and starting all over again. To one waiting for a missionary, you talk about how few girls have the strength of character to wait and how much you admire her for what she's doing. Ask her to show you a picture of her missionary.

My parents were pleased I was dating again and had forgotten about Charly. The trouble was, I hadn't.

I was miserable—a man dying of thirst in the middle of a fresh-water lake.

The crazy thing was that exactly those qualities of Charly's that drove me up the wall were the ones I couldn't forget. After her, talking to any other girl was boring. Charly kept me off balance all the time. Like when we'd be in a restaurant and I'd say, "Please pass the salt," and she'd say, "Well sure, that's easy for you to say." Or when we went once to the University of Utah bookstore and she announced that I was a student at BYU and thought that the U. of U. was one of the most decadent schools in the West, and did anyone there want to argue with me?

The other girls were so predictable—you asked them to pass the salt and they did.

One girl I spent a lot of time with was Kay Randall. We both were studying computer science, and had several classes together. In November, feeling guilty about never having asked her out, I invited her to a movie.

"Let's say you take the worst possible case," she droned on over a piece of pie in a restaurant off-campus after the movie. "Suppose you have a loss-of-cooling accident. What should you do?"

"What?" I asked.

"Aren't you listening?"

"No, you're really boring me," I confessed.

"I thought you'd appreciate my program."

"How about if we go to the airport at Salt Lake and pretend that you've just gotten off a plane from Yugoslavia, can't speak a word of English, and I'm your boyfriend."

"That's a long way to drive for a kiss."

"I don't want to kiss you—I just want some excitement."

"Thanks a lot," she good-naturedly frowned.

"Or how about if we go to a Chinese restaurant and pretend we're spies, and pass secret notes to each other?"

"That sounds really juvenile to me."

"Right—let's be juvenile."

"Why?"

"I'm tired of being mature. It's no fun. Kay, let me ask you a personal question. OK?"

"Well, I guess so."

"Do you have a things-to-do list?"

"That's a personal question? Yes."

"Me, too. And every morning do you write down what you want to accomplish that day, then when you've done it, you check it off the list?"

"Sure, I do that."

"Isn't it terrible?" I groaned.

"I don't see anything terrible about it."

"Don't you? It's ruining our lives." I pulled out my three-by-five card from my shirt pocket. "Here's mine today. 'Do laundry. Put on snow tires. Take Kay out.' At the end of our date, I'm going to put a check beside 'Take Kay out.'"

"So?"

"So you're just one more on the list with dirty clothes and bald tires."

She looked out the window.

"Did you get the snow tires on?"

I looked out and saw the snow falling in large, fluffy flakes.

"It's so beautiful, isn't it?" I sighed. "Just think, the first snow of winter."

"It's going to make driving rotten," she complained.

Suddenly, more than anything in the world, I wanted to be with Charly to enjoy that snowstorm.

Since I couldn't do that, I decided to do what she would have done.

"Hey everybody!" I called out. "Let's all go outside! It's the first snowfall of the season. Why don't we all go out and have a giant snowball fight. How about it, hey!"

The other customers looked at me strangely. Hoping to drum up a little support, I approached a teenage couple, both about sixteen.

"You'd like that, wouldn't you?" I said enthusiastically, leaning over the booth toward them. "We'll go outside and throw snow at each other!"

The girl was obviously terrified, and she melted into her boyfriend's side for protection. He slowly reached one hand toward his steak knife.

I turned to the ones at the counter.

"How about it? This couple's going out with us and we're going to have a lot of fun, throwing snowballs at each other. They're not afraid of doing something spontaneous and fun. Are you?" As I turned to face the couple again, they rushed past me, tossed down some money on the register, and raced to his car. In a few seconds they were gone.

"Oh, I see, you're all too mature for a little snowball fight, is that it?"

No answer. People huddled over their hashed-browns.

"Well, I'm really ashamed of you all."

"What's going on here?" a voice behind me barked.

I turned around to face a policeman.

"I thought it'd be fun if we had a snowball fight," I lamely explained.

"Arrest him!" a little old lady demanded. "He's on dope and he's dangerous."

"I'm not dangerous. I just want to live. Charly would've gone out with me and had a snowball fight."

"Who's Charly?" the cop asked.

"A girl I used to date."

Kay paid our bill and approached the policeman. "I'm with him. Normally he's a very rational person. He's harmless. If you want, I'll make sure he gets home. I'll even drive him home if you'd like."

"You're sure you'll be okay with him?"

"Yes—c'mon, Sam. I'll take you home."

We walked to the jeep. I made the mistake of looking up. Near the light from the street lamp, patterns of snow softly swirled down. A halo of light made each flake look like a saint.

"Nice going, snowflakes," I said quietly.

"Sam, let me drive."

"Nice going, corn plants."

"Sam, give me your keys."

"Nice going, Ferris wheel."

"Sam, the keys. Please—the cop's looking at you funny."

"Nice going, light beams."

"Unless you want to spend the night in jail, quit making eyes at the lamp post!"

I gave her the keys. As she walked to the driver's side, I scooped some snow off the ground and made a snowball. As we left the parking lot, I gently lobbed it toward the restaurant. It hit the window, splashed, and slowly slid down the glass.

She drove me home and then listened to me rattle on about Charly for another hour.

"Kay, I've never asked this of anyone, and I can't ask my parents, but could I borrow some money from you for a few weeks?"

"How much?" she asked.

"Whatever it takes to get to New York and back again."

Chapter Five

I arrived in New York on a Monday afternoon with only thirty dollars in my pocket. The taxi cost twelve dollars, but it put me right in front of Charly's apartment building. Her roommate, a girl majoring in Russian literature, told me Charly had a class, and she drew a little map so I could find it.

I waited outside the classroom for her. By the time she arrived, most of the others had already gone in. She was walking with a guy. I stepped out into the hall to greet her.

"Hi."

She looked at me, frowned, and excused herself from her friend, who went in the classroom.

"What are you doing here?"

"I've changed my mind. I've decided I love you. I want to get married."

"Sam, it's over."

The professor was holding the door open for any latecomers.

"I've got a test this next hour."

"I'll wait for you." The professor closed the door and went in.

"No. Look, it's really over. I don't want to see you again."

A bell rang through the halls, and she started for the door. I followed her. "Just like that? I've come two thousand miles to see you."

She walked into the room and shut the door in front of me.

For a minute I stood looking at the closed door. Then I decided the class was so big that the teacher couldn't know everybody in it. I opened the door, walked over next to Charly, and sat down.

"I love you," I whispered.

"Sam, please, this is an important test."

"Have you been going to church here?"

She nodded her head. The stack of exams came down our row. We each took one.

"Do you think you could get a temple recommend?"

"Class," the professor announced, "I'd like to point out some corrections on the exam paper before you begin. First of all, on page one..."

"See, there was this snowstorm, and I wanted to have all of us at this restaurant go outside and have a snowball fight, but nobody would, and then I realized..."

"I can't hear what he's saying about the exam," she complained.

"And then on page three, there's a very important omission..."

"We could get married at Christmas, or at least the first of the summer."

"I'm not marrying you!"

"Why not?"

"Quit talking or he'll think we're cheating! I'm not talking to you anymore."

With nothing else to do, I looked at the test. Apparently it was a course dealing with marriage and the family, because the first question was an essay question asking for a discussion of the relative advantages and disadvantages of a couple living together without getting married.

"What kind of a dumb class is this?" I whispered.

She shook her head fiercely and wouldn't say anything.

I sat and stared while she chewed her pencil. Her face was beet red and she wasn't writing anything.

"I see you cut your hair," I whispered. "It looks okay. I'm sure I could get used to it."

She turned her whole body away from me and started to write with her paper sideways on the desk.

"How about getting married during Thanksgiving vacation?"

No response.

"There may be some requirement about having to be a member a year before being married in the temple though. So we might have to wait until summer."

No answer.

"Do they have any Ferris wheels open out here this time of year?"

"WILL YOU GET OUT OF HERE?" she yelled. The entire class turned around.

"Only if you promise to talk to me after this stupid exam!"

"I never want to see you again!"

"I won't have you two disrupting my class," the teacher warned us.

"Throw *him* out!" Charly shouted. *"He's* not supposed to be here! He's not even a student at this school! And I didn't ask him here!"

"Well, thanks a lot!"

"Young man, you'd better leave right now!"

I stood up. "I came two thousand miles and I'm not leaving until she agrees to at least talk to me. I want to marry her now. I didn't this summer when she wanted to, but now I do. And I want all you people here to know that I want to get *married.* I don't want to just live with her the way you people in New York do."

Perhaps I could have worded that better.

"What are you talking about?" she screamed. "Nobody's living with me!"

"I meant that in general," I stammered. "I mean, have you all looked at question number one? It asks you to talk about the advantages of living together. I want all you to know that at Brigham Young University there is no question like that!"

The professor whispered something to one of the students, who quickly left the room.

Five minutes later, I was handcuffed and led into the back seat of a police car.

I spent the night in jail, and then they drove me to the airport, put me on the plane, and told me if I ever came back they'd press charges.

At least I didn't have to pay cab fare again.

* * * * *

On the way back in the plane I figured that nobody needed to know about my little adventure. After all, I hadn't really been booked on any charges. There was no reason that anyone in Utah need ever know.

But when I stepped off the plane, my parents and our bishop were there to meet me, which was a surprise.

In half an hour, I was seated beside my bishop in his office.

"It's possible that we may still be able to keep you enrolled at the Y," he began.

As he explained it, there was in Charly's class a member of a bishopric of a Long Island ward. After I had been expelled from class, the professor went on a harangue about Mormons. This good brother stood up to defend the Church, and to assure everyone that not all Mormons were as crazy as me. Afterwards he naturally wanted to know my name. Charly gave it to him. He called his bishop, who phoned BYU, got the name of my campus bishop, talked to him, then phoned my home ward bishop. All this while I sipped my soft drink on the plane.

Over the next hour, Bishop Taylor and I worked out my repentance. It was decided that:

1. I would pay Kay back by dropping a couple of classes and working in the computer center.

2. I would spend my weekends, carefully chaperoned, with my parents in Salt Lake City.

3. I would write the professor in charge of Charly's class and apologize.

4. I would also write and apologize to Charly.

Since I would be home weekends, my dad got me a job doing janitorial work on Saturdays. I was in a huge office, filled with a dozen desks, and when I was there to work, it was completely empty and devoid of life. And that was the way I felt.

After working on Saturday, I would go home, take a shower, and wait for my parents to inform me that a girl and her parents had been invited over for the evening. Somehow I suspected that I had been chosen by some Young Adult group as their service project.

I would sit politely at supper across from the girl appointed for the evening by some committee and we would talk about computers—not because I wanted to, but since I wasn't very talkative, she would invariably ask about my major, I'd tell her, then she'd say that she didn't know any-

34

thing about computers, and I'd begin my canned lecture, putting both me and her to sleep.

One girl was different. I told her that I was majoring in computer science and she said, "That really sounds dull."

"Do you really think so?" I asked, full of hope.

She was a ballet dancer at the U. of U., and I asked about her ankles. They were very strong. She showed me some exercises I could do for mine.

I enjoyed talking to her. I think I even laughed.

Just before she left with her parents, I asked her if she'd go with me to the Ferris wheel. She looked at me strangely, smiled kindly, and said, "Sam, it's winter now—it's closed down."

"I know," I said quietly. "I meant just to look at it."

Her parents, seeing their daughter's plight, quickly changed the conversation, and cheerily and nervously whisked her away.

But I went to the Ferris wheel. Every weekend I spent a few minutes on a cold park bench and stared at the skeleton of the ride. They had stored the chairs inside for the winter, but the frame was still there.

And sometimes when it was snowing hard enough so my parents couldn't see very far into the backyard, I'd go back and stand among the rusted brown stalks and think about Charly.

Then there were my meetings with Bishop Taylor. Each week we talked. He was very kind. I could tell him anything and he would listen and try to help.

Some good came of it. One of the girls from the ward who spent the evening at our home must have written Charly and told her about me, because in early April I got a card from her.

"Sam," she wrote, "I'm sorry to hear you've been having some problems. Sometime I hope we can be friends. Love, Charly."

That got me through the rest of the spring.

At the end of the semester, I moved back in with my parents for the summer, to work at the same job I'd had the previous year.

The first week of June, one of the girls whose project I was called me. "Sam, I found out today that Charly is back in town."

"She is?" I brightened up.

"Yes, but with another guy."

After work that day I drove around her block at least ten times trying to figure out a plan. Nothing came to mind, so I finally just parked and walked to the door.

There were several cars parked in the driveway. Apparently they were having a garden party in back because there was a sign on the door inviting latecomers to just walk in and go through the kitchen to the backyard. I took the sign's advice and eased my way into the kitchen. Through the window, I could see Charly standing next to a business-type person who made his gestures with a pipe in one hand.

"I'll be back in a minute," Charly said as she left and walked into the kitchen. She was halfway through the room before she looked over and saw me.

"Sam?"

"Hi, Charly."

"Good grief, you scared me. For a minute there, I thought you were the ghost of boyfriends past."

"A friend of mine told me you were back. They say it's serious when a girl brings home a guy to meet the parents. Are you engaged?"

"Not officially," she smiled, "but very close. Would you like to meet Mark? He's discovered some very good investment opportunities right here in Utah. Maybe you two could work out a partnership."

The thought of meeting Mark depressed me. "No, I'd better go." Starting for the door, I saw the living room and the mantel and remembered the sunflower seeds and the discussion about her baptism and the thousand other memories of that big box of a room.

I turned back to face her. "I'm sorry for making such a fool of myself in your class. I sent an apology to your teacher."

"Don't worry, it's okay. Can I walk you to your jeep?" We stepped out the front door.

"Whatever happened to all the tickets we got for the Ferris wheel?" she wanted to know.

"I still have some of them," I answered.

"I thought you'd probably use 'em for your other dates."

"Nobody else understands about Ferris wheels." I

paused and then asked, "Have you ever been on a Ferris wheel with Mark?"

"No."

"Oh," I said slowly.

We stood painfully looking at each other.

Finally she broke the spell, touching the hood of the jeep. "Did you ever get this thing out of four-wheel drive?" she asked.

"Sort of—now I can't get it into four-wheel drive." We both smiled faintly.

I decided to go for substance since this was probably our last conversation. "Charly, why didn't you talk to me in New York when I visited you?"

"I don't know, Sam. I should have. You came all that way—I should've talked to you. I guess I was still hurting from the summer. I'm not hurting now."

Walking to the right-hand side of the jeep, I reached in, opened the jockey box, and pulled out several faded tickets.

"There are still a few left," I said, showing them to her.

"I wonder if they're still good," she said pleasantly, looking like her mother with a plastic smile so proper and polite.

"Why do you wonder?"

The veneer disappeared and she quickly added, "I meant that you should find someone else to use them with."

"It'd never be the same, would it? I'll just get rid of them once and for all." I began to rip them up into little pieces.

"Don't!" she said.

Our eyes met.

"Charly, could we go somewhere and talk? Just to make sure things are the way we want them."

"I can't—it's too late."

"Are you married?"

"No."

"Are you engaged?"

"No."

"Then it's not too late. Maybe there's nothing left between us, but don't make me live the rest of my life wondering what would have happened *if*. If there's really nothing left, at least give me the peace of mind of knowing that."

"What do I tell Mark?"

"Leave him a note saying you're going for a ride and you'll explain later."

She went into the house and in a minute was back again. We drove to the park, gave Mr. Raferty the rest of the tickets, and got into the Ferris wheel chair.

"I was listening to Mark through the window while I wrote the note. I think he's talking my dad into buying a duplex for rental income."

"Then the trip out here won't be a waste of time."

"Someday he's going to be the governor of New York. I'm sure of it."

"He has a Word of Wisdom problem."

"You always have to classify people, don't you. Do all Mormons do that?"

"I don't know. You're a Mormon—you tell me."

"Yes, I'm still going to church. That was your next question, wasn't it?"

"Is that where you met Mark?"

"No, he's not LDS, but I've asked him if he'd like to take the lessons."

"What did he say?"

"It's going to take a little work, but he'll come around."

"Are you in love with him?"

"I should be—that's what everyone keeps telling me."

"Well, are you?"

"I have a high regard for him."

"You could say that about your milkman."

"Don't push me, Sam. At least he's never been arrested."

"All I'm asking you is to wait before you do anything dumb like getting engaged to him."

"Why?"

"For starters, he can't take you to the temple. A marriage with him would have a built-in divorce clause."

"So I should marry you just because you can take me to the temple?"

"Look, if it's not going to work out between us, just say the word and I'll introduce you to about forty returned missionaries who are eligible. Pick one of them to take you to the temple, but don't marry out of the church."

"You sound like a bishop."

"Charly, I haven't been able to forget you. Maybe at first

you loved me more, but I've had a year to catch up. Give me another chance."

She started to rummage through her old leather bag. "You never can find anything when you need it. I put tissues in here, and they're around for months, but the minute I want one, they all disappear."

"I have a clean handkerchief," I volunteered.

She wiped her eyes and blew her nose. "Tomorrow night my mother is throwing another party. She knows I haven't said yes to Mark yet, but she's trying to talk me into making an engagement announcement at the party. She even has a cake ordered that will say, 'Best Wishes for a Life Together.' And you know she's not that fond of you. So what do we do about that?"

"Cake will freeze for months. Put it in the freezer until you decide."

"What about Mark?"

"I don't think you should put him in the freezer, but it's up to you."

Just then we heard somebody arguing with Mr. Raferty. It was Mark. Charly scrunched down in her chair, but he'd already seen her.

"I want this thing stopped! He's kidnapped her!"

"I'm not stopping anything until their ride's up. They've got ten more rides left, and that's what they're going to get."

Mark stormed away to a pay phone and made two phone calls.

"Charly, what did your note say?"

"I just said I was being taken for a ride. Is that bad?"

"Not usually, but he thinks you've been kidnapped. He probably found the torn-up tickets and came here."

Mark hurried back to the Ferris wheel and began arguing again with Mr. Raferty.

On our way down, Charly tried to explain, but Mark lunged for me, missed, didn't get away in time, and was struck on the shoulder by part of the frame. The blow threw him against Mr. Raferty. They both fell down and in the process broke off the speed control lever.

We started going fast. I put my arms around Charly and held her close. If I hadn't been scared, I would have enjoyed it more.

Raferty was unconscious, but Mark got up, looked around, grabbed a long pole, and crammed it into the gear mechanism. The pole jerked out of his hand, throwing him to the ground and knocking him out. Suddenly the pulley for the drive mechanism snapped and the Ferris wheel slowed down and stopped.

Less than a minute later, the police arrived, apparently called by Mark from the pay phone. A police ambulance took Mark and Mr. Raferty to the hospital.

Then Charly's mother and father arrived.

She leaned over to tell them that everything was okay, but the motion caused one of the light panels to fall to the ground. The police told us to be quiet and not to move around.

One of the policemen grabbed a bullhorn and summoned me. "I want you to throw down the weapon you used against the operator and this girl's boyfriend. I don't want you harming the girl."

"No, I don't ever want to do that," I whispered in her ear.

"You've already got a charge of kidnapping against you. Don't make it any worse. Throw down the weapon."

"Sam, you're not cooperating," she teased.

"I don't have a weapon."

"Let's see if I can help." She opened her bag and we sifted through the contents. Finally we found a pair of pinking shears, which we tossed down. It seemed to please everyone.

In a few minutes a fire truck with ladder pulled close to us.

"Miss, just reach slowly and grab hold of my hand. I'll have you down in no time," the fireman on the extended ladder said.

"If I jumped, that'd be getting down in no time. Let's take it slow. See you, Sam."

In a minute I was back down on the ground, too. After Charly talked to the police and we called the hospital and had Mr. Raferty explain things, they undid the handcuffs.

On our way to the hospital with her parents, Charly explained that she probably would get engaged, but not at the party the next day, and maybe not to Mark.

"But what about the cake?" her mother asked.

"Freeze it," we answered in unison.
That's just what we did.

Chapter Six

The one thing Charly didn't lack in making a decision about marriage was advice. From morning until evening, somebody was telling her what to do. Her mother was especially active in promoting Mark as the best choice. For my part, I made sure that our new bishop, Bishop Archer, talked to her about the importance of temple marriage.

"How are you going to decide which of us to marry?" I asked her once as the three of us sipped lemonade on her patio.

"Would it be possible for me to see how each of you react to practical situations that occur in a marriage, such as handling children?"

"Sounds boring," Mark said.

"I think it's a terrific idea!" I countered, relying on my church background to have prepared me for family life.

The first little exercise involved taking a child to the zoo for the afternoon. Mark and Charly took the daughter of the man who came in once a week to tend Charly's parents' lawn. It went quite well, according to Mark. On the next day, she and I took the man's five-year-old son, Lee.

We had no more than entered the zoo when Lee wanted an ice cream cone—which I bought him. A few feet later, he wanted a stuffed lion—which I bought him.

By the time we reached where they kept the real lions, I was definitely ready to feed Lee to them.

"I want a balloon! I want a balloon!" he cried as he saw a man selling helium-filled balloons.

"Sam, he wants a balloon."

"All right," I replied, approaching the balloon man. "How much are the balloons?"

"Three dollars."

"Are you kidding? Forget it." I walked back to Charly and Lee. "Hey, little fella, the balloons here cost too much. Be a good boy and I'll get you one at a store after we leave the zoo."

"I want a balloon now!"

"You did say you'd buy him a balloon," Charly said tensely.

"For three dollars? Are you crazy?"

"Look at all the other people who bought their children a balloon," she chided.

"I can't help it if other people are foolish with their money."

"I want a balloon!"

"All right, you little brat, I'll get you a balloon!"

I marched to the balloon man. "Give me a balloon," I snarled.

"What color?"

"I don't care."

He gave me a brown balloon. Grudgingly, I tossed the money down and stomped back, thrusting the balloon at the boy.

"Here's your balloon. I hope you're satisfied now."

He looked at it for a second and then burst into tears again. "I don't want a brown balloon. I want a red one!"

In disgust, he let go of the balloon. I jumped up to get it before it floated away. When I came down, I landed on top of Lee's ice cream cone, smearing chocolate ice cream on my mint green slacks.

"You broke my ice cream cone! And I want a red balloon!"

"He has his little heart set on a red balloon! Is that asking too much?" Charly demanded.

"Why do you always take the kid's side?" I asked sharply, trying to wipe the chocolate stain from my slacks with a handkerchief.

"And why can't you remember his name?"

"I want a red balloon!"

"Sam, he's upsetting the lions! Give him what he wants!"

"All right," I grumbled, marching back to the balloon man. "I'd like to exchange my brown balloon for a red balloon."

"Sorry, we don't take exchanges. If you want a red balloon, it'll be another three dollars."

I glared at Charly, deliberately released the brown balloon into the air, picked out a red balloon, and tied it on Lee's wrist, wondering all the while how many it would take to make him float away.

"How long you folks been married?" the balloon man asked.

"Why?" I asked.

"You'd better get some marriage counseling. Your marriage is in trouble. I'd rather clean out the elephant cage than be with you two for very long."

"Who asked you?" Charly growled.

As we started toward the next exhibit, Lee began again. "I want another ice cream cone."

The whole experience gave us a new perspective into family life.

* * * * *

Charly still hadn't made up her mind, so she suggested another activity, which she labeled Buying Food for a Family. We'd each go as a couple and buy a week's worth of groceries without spending over thirty dollars.

I wanted to ask her if she was keeping a graph, but didn't for fear that she was and that I'd find out how poorly I was doing compared to Mark.

Again, Mark and Charly went first and had no trouble.

I was absolutely sure I would be able to handle this, since I had done virtually the same thing for two years on my mission.

It wasn't until later that we found out Mark had hired a detective agency to sabotage my efforts by slipping extra items in the cart when I wasn't looking and also by changing the price tags of items after I had put them into the cart.

I should have suspected something as we made our way through the store. We were stopped three times to be given free samples of new brands of chocolate milk, potato chips, and tomato soup. In addition, we were involved in two collisions, during which time people were altering what was in my cart. Unfortunately, we didn't suspect a thing.

It was a busy Saturday afternoon. We waited for ten minutes before we could get checked out, and behind us six other people were in line.

"We'll even have enough left over for a treat," I confidently told Charly as I checked the figure on my portable calculator, on which I had added the prices.

"Ground chuck at three dollars and ninety-three cents per pound. Total, eight dollars and forty-three cents," the exhausted checkout lady rattled off.

I was horrified. "Excuse me, but I think you must've read the price wrong—this is hamburger."

She handed me the package. "See for yourself."

I looked at the price, dumbfounded. "Well, I'll admit that's what it says, but I'm sure that's not the price."

She shrugged her shoulders. "All I do is read the price on the package."

I sent Charly back to the meat counter to get another package of hamburger. The people waiting behind us grumbled at the delay.

The checkout girl picked up the next item. "One large bottle of caviar—fifteen dollars."

"I don't want caviar!" I exclaimed.

"Then don't put it in your cart!" she snapped.

"I didn't put it in my cart. It's not even on my list."

"Hey, hurry up," the lady behind us said. "You gonna argue about everything?"

"Imported coconut wine sauce, five dollars and twenty-nine cents."

In desperation, I threw my body across the cart. "Stop! I want to check my cart."

The checkout girl muttered under her breath.

I started to dig through the cart, pulling out several unwanted items. "I don't want this, and I don't want this."

"Why do all the nuts shop on Saturday when it's busy?" the man fourth in line asked the lady in front of him.

"Are you through now?" the checkout girl asked.

"Yes, I am. Go ahead."

"All right. Detergent, twelve dollars a box."

"Stop!"

"Do you want detergent or not?" she yelled.

"Yes, but the price went up!"

"The price is always going up!"

"I mean, the price went up since I put it in my cart!"

By this time, the manager was there.

"Sam, I'll pay for it," Charly offered, "let's just get out of here."

"Somebody in this store is out to make sure I spend more than thirty dollars!" I announced.

"You ever hear of inflation?" the checkout girl asked.

The bill came to fifty-eight dollars.

* * * * *

To this day, I'm not sure why Charly finally decided to marry me instead of Mark.

It certainly wasn't because her parents approved of me. Mark was everything they had ever wanted. Educated at Columbia, he already had financial holdings. He was witty and his little New York accent was endearing—he sounded like John Kennedy with a chest cold. He played an excellent game of bridge and golf.

We played Charly's little family exercises for an entire week. After Going to the Zoo, and Buying Food for a Family, there was Helping in the Kitchen (Mark turned out to be an excellent chef compared to me and my hamburger slosh dish), and Budgeting our Finances. In every case Mark had done as well as or better than I had. So when I showed up at her house one day ready to play another game, I was surprised to hear that Mark had gone home.

"I'm not going to marry him."

"Oh," I said. "Does this mean you're going to take me up on the offer to introduce you to forty returned missionaries?"

"No, that won't be necessary, thank you."

"Oh," I said, wondering if she had decided to go on a mission.

"I've decided to marry you."

"You have? Why?"

"I prayed about it."

Ever since Charly was one year old, her mother had been making plans for a spectacular wedding, complete with bridesmaids, flowergirls, ring bearers, rose petal throwers—the whole circus.

For me, though, there was only one place to get married

and that was in the temple. Consequently, when her parents, still heartbroken about losing Mark, finally understood what we wanted, they were not pleased.

"You mean to tell us that you want to get married in a place where we can't even be there to watch?" her father asked.

"You can be at the reception," I suggested.

He gave me a withering look. "I'm just shocked that you'd want to hurt your mother like this. You're her only child, and you'd deny her the satisfaction of seeing you being married."

"Daddy, I don't want to hurt anyone. It's just that Sam and I want to be married for time and eternity."

"What does that mean?" her mother asked.

"We want to be married even after we die," I tried to explain. "You two aren't, you know. When one of you dies, your marriage is null and void because you were only married 'until death do you part.' "

"Can't you go through the temple after you've been married civilly?" her mother asked.

"Yes," I admitted, "but we'd have to wait a year—and besides, we don't want a civil marriage."

"Why not? You believe it's legal, don't you?"

"Sure, but it's a cheap imitation of the real thing."

Her mother flinched.

"You both are being selfish, only thinking of yourselves, aren't you? What about your mother? Doesn't she deserve any consideration? Are you going to shut her out of your own wedding?"

Charly started to cry. That got her mother going, and she left the room in tears. Her father mixed himself a drink. I ate a few cocktail nuts, left conveniently on the coffee table. It looked like this was going to be messy, since I knew I wasn't going to compromise.

A few minutes later, Charly's mother returned, red-eyed but composed. "John," she said softly, touching her husband's arm, "it's their marriage and their wedding. They should have it just the way they want it."

That was the first time I kissed my mother-in-law.

Chapter Seven

We had our interviews with the bishop and stake president only ten days before the wedding date. As far as I could tell, the interviews had gone well. At least, on our way home that night, we both had temple recommends in hand. But Charly was strangely quiet as we pulled up in front of her house.

"Anything wrong?" I asked, turning off the motor.

She took a deep breath and closed her eyes. "Sam, before I joined the Church, or even knew anything about it, there were some problems in my life, problems that would've prevented me from getting a temple recommend if I'd been a member of the Church. I thought I should tell you."

"What kind of problems?"

She nervously pursed her lips. "Problems of moral cleanliness."

I felt sick.

"Did you tell the bishop and stake president about it?"

"I told them everything."

"And they still gave you a recommend?"

"Sam, it was before I even had heard about the Church—in New York."

"Why didn't you tell me about this sooner?"

"When I was baptized, you told me my past sins were completely forgiven."

I couldn't let it alone. "Do you remember all their names?" I asked, tortured by my imagination.

She started to cry. "Doesn't it make any difference to you that since I've been baptized I've kept the commandments?"

"I don't want used merchandise."

I could just as well have struck her in the face—it would have hurt her less.

"I'm sorry!" I apologized, seeing the look of devastation on her face.

We sat in the dark, silent except for her tears. Then I walked her to the door and left. Just before I got into the jeep, she called my name and I turned around.

"The announcements are already mailed," she said.

"I know."

"What should I do?"

"I don't know."

"Should I start phoning to cancel it?"

"No . . . not yet."

I drove to Bishop Archer's office.

"Bishop, I can't marry her. She told me what happened before she joined the Church."

"She has completely repented."

"She's not clean in my eyes and she never will be."

With great patience he went through several scriptures dealing with repentance and forgiveness, but they didn't seem to help me.

"Bishop, I don't care about that. You never should've given her that recommend. She's not pure the way I want my wife to be. She's not worthy."

He raised his bushy eyebrows. "You really feel that way?"

"Yes, I do."

"Then give me your recommend, please."

I handed it to him and he put it in his desk drawer.

"What did you do that for?" I complained. "She's the one, not me."

He stood up to usher me out of his office.

"Why did you take my recommend away?"

"You don't believe in the atonement of the Savior! Until you do—until you can accept that people can make mistakes and repent and receive forgiveness—you'll never get a temple recommend from me."

"You don't understand."

"I could understand if you said you couldn't marry her because you personally couldn't deal with her past, but I won't let you tell me she's not worthy, because that simply isn't true."

"You had no right to take away my recommend. I answered all the questions right."

"I'm the bishop of this ward and a judge in Israel. And I say that she's more worthy than you are. Don't you call unclean what the Lord has pronounced clean!" And with that, he closed his office door.

I stormed to the stake president's house and demanded that he release the bishop. He asked me why, I told him, and after I did, he replied that he would have done the same thing and that I was the one in need of repentance.

I spent the next several hours driving and thinking and, later, after my anger had subsided, praying.

Did I believe in the atonement of the Savior? Yes. Did I believe that baptism could produce a washing away of past sins? Yes. Did I believe that Charly had lived the commandments after her baptism? Yes.

Then what was the problem? I could believe that the Savior could forget past sins—but I wasn't sure I could. What if I were forever haunted by bitter fantasies about her past? How could I ever forget that I, if we did get married, wasn't the first?

About two in the morning, I parked my jeep on a barren ridge and prayed for help. Then I sat in the jeep and thought.

What if I had never heard about the Church until I was the age she had been when she moved to Utah? What if, when I was growing up, there had been no Sunday School or seminary or Mutual or firesides or bishop's interviews? What mistakes would I have made?

All of them, I realized.

I reflected back on the day Charly came out of the waters of baptism—the glow that filled her face. And our conversation in the garden the week after her baptism. And the changes I had seen in her as she learned about church standards. She had gradually made changes in every aspect of her life—even to the point of altering her sleeveless dresses so she'd be able to wear them after going through the temple. Day by day, she had become a new person, inside and out.

That was it! She had become a new person!

The fear and misgivings left me, and I wanted to be with her and apologize and let her know that I loved her and wasn't troubled anymore. I drove as fast as I dared down the mountain, but by the time I arrived at her house, it was three-thirty in the morning.

At first I tried to throw little pebbles against her window, but they didn't wake her, so I proceeded to throw progressively larger pebbles.

It's hard to judge these things. The sixth rock shattered her window, making a terrific crash.

I heard her father shouting for his wife to call the police. Then the lights in the two bedrooms flickered on. In a second, he stuck his head out a window.

"What's going on out there?"

"Good morning, Father," I sweetly answered.

He swore and left the window, muttering Charly's name. In a minute, she was leaning out.

"Sam?"

"Yeah. Hi."

"Did you say Father?"

"Yeah. Does he prefer that or should I call him Dad?"
Silence.

"Charly, I love you more than ever. I'm sorry for being so unkind to you. You are virtuous and good and clean and I love you."

"I love you, too. It's almost morning, isn't it? Do you want some breakfast?"

"Sure, let's have an almost-breakfast, shall we?"

* * * * *

We were married on a Friday in July in the Salt Lake Temple. That evening there was a reception in which we wore out our smiling muscles.

Then we had one last dish of ice cream with our parents at her home.

"Sam," her father cornered me beside the jeep as I threw in Charly's suitcase, "if you ever need any help—a loan or anything—don't hesitate to let me know." Tears were forming in his eyes, and that surprised me.

"Thanks, but I want to be as independent as I can. I don't think we'll be needing anything, but thank you anyway."

Her mother's stenciled-on face was starting to melt

51

from the tears she'd unloosed that day. I'm sure there were mascara erosion lines around her eyes.

"Mom, thanks for letting me go to the temple," Charly cried when it was time to leave them. "Someday you'll understand why it was so important to me." She threw her arms around her mother and they both sobbed. It made me feel like the wicked ogre tearing the fair young maiden from her parents and home.

Charly was still crying as I drove the few miles to the Hotel Utah. I, on the other hand, whistled a happy, although nervous, tune.

Approaching the reservation desk, I boldly announced, "My wife and I have a reservation. The name's Roberts."

He looked at us—probably no differently than he looked at anyone else, but it made me feel embarrassed and, yes, guilty.

"Do you want to see our marriage license?" I said, my voice cracking.

He smiled. "No sir, that won't be necessary."

It seemed unusual to be changing into newly purchased pajamas that evening as Charly prepared herself in the bathroom. As I nervously tried to find all the pins the factory had hidden in the pajamas, I recalled my mission president explaining his feelings about being on a mission: "There's no place in the world I'd rather be than where I am right now." Except for my nervousness, and my fear of leaving one pin in the pajamas, that was the way I felt at that moment.

When she came out, she looked so beautiful in her long, white, flowing, modest negligee.

"Well," she said quietly, "here we are." She sat on the bed beside me. Nervously I cleared my throat.

"Hello, husband dear," she said with a slight smile.

"Before we begin," I said, borrowing an old missionary line, "we'd like to have a word of prayer."

We did, too, a kneeling prayer—our first family prayer.

Chapter Eight

That fall we moved to Provo so I could finish my last semester of school. We must have examined every ratty basement apartment in the city, looking for a bargain. Even though we were poor, I had refused all offers of aid from our parents.

"Where's the shower?" I asked one landlord as we peered into the cramped bathroom.

"It's in the kitchen."

We didn't believe him so we looked. Sticking out of the wall was a shower spout and on the floor was a drain. A flimsy sheet hung down for privacy.

"It works okay—just remember to mop up after every shower."

Of course, it wasn't in any list of approved housing, but it was cheap. We took it. After all, it was only going to be for one semester.

The entire apartment was an afterthought. You walked into it and found yourself in a narrow hall. The ceiling was crammed with heat ducts for the people upstairs. In the middle of the apartment was a room containing the furnace and hot water heater. The living room consisted of one plastic couch, a coffee table, and a lawn chair. In the bedroom was the bed and that was about all. There was a closet about the size of a phone booth. The kitchen was on the other side of the furnace room, close to the entrance door. The whole apartment was painted in a happy, light-hearted brown.

The landlord and his wife lived above us with their four healthy boys. We got to know them all quite well, listening to their conversation over our heads and hearing them clomp around. We soon could recognize each of them by his walk. We only hoped we weren't as noticeable to them.

In order to get by, I took a job at the computer center part-time, and Charly became an Avon lady.

One October Saturday afternoon, after spending a disappointing day leaning over the jeep trying to fix it without spending any money, I was taking a shower to wash away all the grease. I had turned off the water and was soaping down when I heard a knock on the door. Charly answered it.

"Mom and Dad, what a surprise!"

Not wishing to be discovered naked in my kitchen, I grabbed a towel and ran to the bedroom to dress. I still had globs of soap on my body, and since I couldn't rinse it off, I tried to wipe it off. Finally dressed, anxious to get back to the kitchen and clean up after the shower, I started out of the bedroom only to remember that my hair was full of soap. I grabbed an old fishing cap, plopped it on my head, and raced to the kitchen.

Charly had devised a clever way to hide the shower. We hid the curtain in a drawer, hung a pot of flowers from the nozzle, and placed two blue baby booties over the hot and cold water handles. I had completed that procedure and was madly mopping when Charly ushered her parents into the kitchen.

"Sam, isn't this a surprise?" she said, rolling her eyes for my benefit.

"It certainly is."

"I think it's admirable that you help out in the house," my mother-in-law said.

"Oh, I do this several times a week," I truthfully replied.

"Let's all go sit down in the living room," Charly suggested.

We walked single file to the couch. Her father banged his head on one of the heat ducts along the way. Her parents sat down on the couch, Charly sat in the lawn chair, and I casually leaned against the wall.

"Have you got the flu?" her father asked me.

"No, why?"

"Your face is sweating so," he answered, no doubt observing the water trickling down my face from my wet hair. "And why are you wearing that cap in the house?"

"Oh, this?" I chuckled. "It's just an old fishing cap. I don't even know I have it on most of the time."

One of the boys began to bounce a golf ball on the floor above us. Charly's parents stared at our ceiling.

"You'll stay for supper, won't you?" Charly bravely asked.

"Oh no, we don't want to interfere. Look, don't think we're checking up on you. We were just in the area and thought we'd drop in. But we're definitely not staying for supper."

That's a relief, I thought to myself.

"Nonsense, you stay. It's on the stove, there's plenty, and I'll have it ready in no time."

We were having pinto beans and day-old bread.

By this time the drying, caked-on soap was itching me to distraction. I began to scratch incessantly.

"I can hardly taste the ham," her father quietly announced to his wife after trying the beans.

"Oh, there's no ham in it," Charly explained. "You see, we feel that the bean itself has such a delicate flavor that adding ham would ruin it. Would you like some more milk?" she asked, nearly ready to refill their glasses with frothy, chalky, freshly made powdered milk.

"No, thank you," they said in unison.

Then one of the boys upstairs started to practice his trombone. We were used to it, but to her parents it must have sounded like we were living in a foghorn.

I was scratching to beat the band—well, at least in time with the trombone march tune.

"Don't you ever take off that hat?" her father snapped.

Charly reached over and removed it, revealing a caked white layer over my entire head.

"Good grief!" her father gasped. "That's the worst dandruff problem I've ever seen. No wonder you wear a hat."

Her mother indirectly asked Charly if I had infected her with the same scalp disease, and encouraged her to buy something at the drugstore as a preventive for herself.

The boys started to wrestle directly above us.

Charly's mother began to cry.

I continued to scratch.

Suddenly the fight upstairs ended with the sound of shattering glass. The father, who had been outside working on his car, stomped into the house and across the floor overhead.

"Now what have you done?" he yelled.

"David and Jimmy were fighting and broke the light!" the trombone player explained.

"How many times do I have to tell you—don't fight in the house!"

"He started it!" a voice complained.

"I didn't either!"

As I looked about, I realized that all of us were staring at the ceiling and listening to the family drama above us. In a few minutes it was over. Our landlord went back outside and in his rage revved up his car engine over and over again—of course the car was just outside our window. One of the boys bounced the golf ball again, this time dropping it and then letting it bounce over and over again until it came to rest.

"Oh, what a pretty hanging basket of flowers," Charly's mother gamely said, trying to be brave and say something nice about the apartment. "And look at this, John. What is it? A booty sculpture?"

"Don't touch that!" we both yelled.

Our yelling frightened Mom, who already had her hand on one handle. The shower spouted forth in a spray that caught us all. I jumped for the handle and turned it off.

"What is that?" her father roared.

"It's our shower."

They looked at the shower, and then at the kitchen stove, and then at me. I knew what they were thinking—imagining Charly busily cooking supper while I stood three feet from her taking a shower. Tacky, tacky, tacky.

On their way out, her father said, "Monday morning, I'm setting up a checking account for you two. Let me help until you're through school, and then you can pay me back."

"No, thanks, we're getting along fine."

"This is not fine," he said, glancing back. "And I don't like the idea of my daughter walking the streets peddling perfume."

"I don't want your money. I wasn't interested in it when we got married, and I'm not interested in it now."

"She's my daughter. I don't want her getting sick because she's not eating right."

"We're doing all right, but even if we weren't I wouldn't take a dime from you."

Her mother hated to leave Charly alone with me and

whatever disease I had that caused me to scratch like a monkey. She was still crying when she left, and by that time her father wasn't even speaking to me.

Monday morning we received an anonymous canned ham in the mail.

*　*　*　*　*

In many ways the best times we had were in those poor days in our married-student ward. Several of us had been married the previous summer and we had everything in common. We spent nearly every Saturday evening with one or two other couples playing Monopoly and eating popcorn or attending a free campus activity.

But as time passed, some differences began to become obvious. Many of the other wives became pregnant, but Charly didn't.

Chapter Nine

In January I took a job as a computer programmer for a consulting engineering firm in Rapid City, South Dakota. Basically there were two reasons for my taking the job: It paid reasonably well and was something I could do—and it got us away from our parents.

My parents: "Well, I don't see my grandchild coming along yet." Sometimes our failure at this would cause Charly to cry and wonder if Heavenly Father didn't trust us with a child.

Her parents: "You should be doing more with your life than just being a wife. You've got a good mind—you should develop a career for yourself."

And I would say, "We believe the place of the wife is in the home."

Her mother would say, "Whatever for?"

So we moved seven hundred miles away to be by ourselves.

Rapid City is located on the edge of the Black Hills. The Chamber of Commerce bills it as the banana belt, but if that's true, you're talking about cold bananas. At least that was the way it seemed in January. There wasn't much snow, but the wind blew with a fierceness we had never seen before.

After a few months of apartment living, we began to look for a house to buy, but the whole thing seemed like an exercise in futility when we found out what sort of down payments they wanted. There was no way we would ever be able to come up with that kind of money.

"But Sam, I want to be in our own home and be like all

the other dull wives," Charly said one evening just before we went to bed.

"We can't afford it."

"I talked to my father today. He said he'd loan us the down payment at no interest. We could pay it back a little at a time."

"No," I said automatically.

"Why not?"

"I don't want to be sponging from your father."

"It's just a loan—we'll pay it back. C'mon, Sam, he loves us and wants to help out. It's his only pleasure in life."

"No."

"Do you know what's wrong with you?" she asked, energetically brushing her hair. "You can give help to others, but you can't accept anything, can you?"

"No, I can't. Besides that, I know your parents didn't think much of me when we got married, and if we took money from them, it would just confirm their opinion."

"Sam, I think you're wrong about this."

"I'm the priesthood leader in the home, and I say no."

"But you haven't even prayed about it, have you?"

"I don't need to."

Before we got into bed, I asked her to give the prayer.

" . . . and bless Sam so he'll know that even though it is more blessed to give than to receive, that it is sometimes blessed to receive—so we can move into a home and be able to follow our prophet's advice to have a garden, and so children can come to us, and they'll have a decent place to play, providing Thou wilt help us get pregnant . . ."

I couldn't help it. I started to laugh.

"All right! What's going on here?" Charly demanded, faking anger. "I'm trying to say a nice little prayer and you're laughing. What's Heavenly Father going to think about that?"

She grabbed a pillow and began to hit me with it.

"You rotten husband, that's for being irreverent, and that's for being such a hard-headed man . . ."

To protect myself, I kissed her.

The prayer stayed on hold for a long time.

* * * * *

Gradually, over the next few weeks, Charly patiently kept on giving me reasons why it would be smart to accept her father's offer to loan us the down payment for a house. She must have spent hours at the library reading books and magazine articles about what a wise investment a home could be as a hedge against inflation. She set up a monthly pay-back schedule for the loan from her father.

Finally I swallowed my pride and admitted she was right. The check was in the mail to us that very day.

Now we looked at houses with new enthusiasm, but eventually we had to swallow the fact that "our price range" would only allow a little cracker box of a house. Then we met a salesman who told us how we could get "more house for the money" by doing some of the finishing work ourselves. The more of the finishing we did, the more we would save. He drove us around to happy, smiling families who told us how simple it had been for them to do the uncomplicated jobs like plumbing, wiring, putting up sheet rock, and taping and texturing. They made it sound easy, and we became entranced with the idea of getting the house we wanted rather than the one we could afford.

Eventually we bought a piece of land in one of the canyons a few miles from the town. We were surrounded by trees and hills; our nearest neighbor was a quarter of a mile away.

We subcontracted out the digging and the pouring of the foundation as well as the framing and roofing. I reserved everything else for myself.

Work couldn't start until April because of the weather, but by the end of June the workmen were through. In order to save money, we left our apartment, bought a tent, and moved onto our land. The first thing I built was an outhouse to serve us until I got the plumbing in. We already had a power utility pole near the house, and by stringing a cord to a hot plate, Charly was able to cook.

By the end of August, the novelty of camping had worn off.

* * * * *

It was a Tuesday morning in September. By then we had moved our mattress inside, into what would one day be the bedroom, but at that time was just a series of two-by-four studs outlining where the walls would be. We draped some old sheets around the studs to give us some semblance of privacy and hung our clothes from a rope tied to the studs. Our bed was just the mattress on the rough wood floor. By then I had the electrical wiring done, but was still waiting for the man to do the digging for our septic tank. We didn't have any plumbing.

"Charly, do you need the car for Relief Society?" I asked, wondering if she wanted to drive me to work so she could have the car.

"No," she said sleepily. "I don't think I'll go today."

"Oh, why not?"

"I don't want to go."

"Is anything wrong?"

"I just don't want to go."

I didn't think much more about it until Saturday evening after both of us had worked all day on the house.

"If we worked tomorrow," she suggested, "we could get twice as much done."

"You mean not go to church?"

"Yes, that's exactly what I mean."

We were looking at each other over a crude table that also served as a carpentry bench. Her face was streaked with dirt, and there was dust and sawdust in thick piles across the floor.

"We can't miss church, can we?"

"Sam, at the rate you're going, we're going to freeze out here before very long."

"But what about my Sunday School class?"

"They can get someone else, can't they?"

"Is something wrong?"

"Everything's wrong! Haven't you noticed?"

"Like what?"

"Like I'm sick of wading through five inches of dirt! I'm tired of having to get up in the middle of the night and walk to an outhouse! I'm sick of sleeping on the floor and looking at boards where a wall should be. I'm sick of this whole thing. If you wanted a noble wife, someone to pull your handcart with you, you picked the wrong girl!"

"Oh, you'll feel better after you've had a shower," I said comfortingly.

"Don't tell me how I'm going to feel! Also I'm sick of

walking into somebody's house and imposing on them to use their bathroom so I can clean myself up."

"They don't mind."

"But I do. Sam, let's get this place finished. Let's not go to church until it is."

"We belong in church."

"Then why won't they help us?" she complained bitterly. "They all know the way we're living here. Why hasn't anybody asked if they could help?"

Sheepishly I met her gaze, and then she knew.

"You've told them we don't need any help, haven't you! They've offered, but you wouldn't accept it!"

She threw her dish of pork and beans on the floor and stomped away. I got up and followed her. There was no place in the house she could shut me out, but she went into the bedroom and tried to pin the sheet so I couldn't get in. I just walked between the studs, which made her furious. She pounded her fists on my chest and yelled, *"Why* can't you accept help?"

To calm her down, I promised, "I'll have the plumbing done by next week."

"I don't believe you anymore! That's what you said last week and the week before that. Sam, I can't take this any longer."

The rest of the evening was like living in an ice plant. We were both locked into a tremendously intricate game, and as much as we wanted to, we couldn't seem to get out of it. The rules of this game were that we must not show affection, that we must remain distant, and that we must refrain from communication except about trivial matters.

I worked late into the night and she went to bed early.

The next morning I got up early and studied my Sunday School lesson before priesthood meeting. She came out wearing jeans and a sweatshirt a little before I had to go.

"I'll drive you to church so I'll have the car today."

"What for?"

"I'm going to take a drive in the hills."

"Oh."

We drove silently to church. As we pulled into the parking lot and stopped, I looked at her, hoping we could say something.

"Sam, we're just like all the other unhappily married couples now, aren't we?"

"I guess we are. I'm sorry."

"For what?"

I tapped the steering wheel with my fist. "That's just it. I don't know. What should I be sorry for?"

"Are you sorry you married me?" she asked painfully.

"No. How about you?"

"I don't know. I feel so out of place. I wake up in the morning, look around at the mess, and ask myself how I got here. Sam, maybe you should've married someone from Utah who was born in the Church."

"No, I love you."

I picked up my lesson materials and walked into the building alone.

Our poor bishop—all he asked when he met me in the hall was, "How's it going, Sam?" I followed him into the office, sat down, and asked, "Do you really want to know?"

Once again I became the object of a service project. The next Saturday morning at seven o'clock, there were fifteen men and boys at our door.

By four o'clock they were gone, like a tornado in reverse—one that creates order. Solemnly Charly and I walked into the bathroom to look at our toilet. She started to cry, and then we sat down on the floor and with great love caressed its gleaming white surface and flushed and cried and flushed some more.

*　*　*　*　*

After that, for a while at least, we became civilized. We had rooms and doors and in a while carpeting and a stove. We didn't have any living room furniture—we were too poor for that. But we could lounge around on our thick carpet and talk. It was wonderful. The day we moved the outhouse building away a few feet and filled in the pit was a great occasion. On an impulse we poured gasoline on the wooden structure and burned it to the ground while Charly did a dance around it. It was a good thing our neighbors were not close.

Shortly after that, Charly was asked to substitute teach a Relief Society class dealing with home management. She had always been a little wary of Relief Society because the sisters all seemed to be so much better qualified in the home than she was. So she fretted over the lesson for days, reading book after book about homemaking skills. Finally, a few days before Relief Society, she read back to me the various quotations she had gleaned from her studies.

"Well, what do you think about it?"

"It's very informative," I said, trying to be tactful.

"Is it that bad?" she moaned.

"Charly, who do you want to reach in your lesson?"

"Reach? I just want to get it over with."

"I mean, are you trying to impress all the other women in the ward with how accomplished you are in homemaking?"

"Is that what it sounds like? They all know how bad I am—that I have to call up for instructions to sew a button on a shirt. What are you trying to tell me?"

"You just need to decide who you want to reach."

She puzzled over that all night. Finally, about two in the morning, she woke me up. "I know who I want to reach. I want to reach me. I want the sisters who are just beginning to come out to feel comfortable with Relief Society and want to come all the time."

"Ohhh," I mumbled before falling asleep again.

She gave the lesson her way, and from all I've heard, it was a hit. She gave some *basic* homemaking hints that she had used herself. For example: If you like to sleep in late, but feel guilty when somebody calls at ten-thirty and asks if she got you out of bed—then simply plug in a vacuum cleaner next to your bed, and just before answering the phone, turn it on. After saying hello, tell the caller to wait a minute while you turn it off. You may also want to tape some kitchen cleaning sounds to play back while you lounge in bed and talk on the phone.

After the lesson a recent convert, Sister Ritter, came up and joked with Charly, and then confided that she also sometimes felt inadequate around some of the other women, who all seemed to be so much better than she was.

"But I don't feel that way about you," Sister Ritter confided.

They talked through the luncheon. Brother and Sister Ritter were in their mid-fifties and had joined the Church a little over six months ago in another stake. For their entire marriage they had drifted from city to city—partly because of a drinking problem that her husband had.

"Sometimes he still drinks," she confided to Charly, "but he's working on it, and as soon as he quits, he's going to start coming out to church again."

"That's backwards," Charly said. "He needs to come out to church so he'll have the strength to quit."

"He wouldn't feel comfortable there. He doesn't know anybody."

"He will. You both are invited for supper tomorrow night. I'm cooking Sam's favorite."

"What's that?"

"To tell you the truth, I don't know. I guess anything that's not burnt."

They came. During the course of the evening Brother Ritter became increasingly fidgety until Charly figured out why.

"Could I talk to you alone, Brother Ritter?" she asked.

They went outside and talked so he could have a cigarette. When he came back, he was better.

From that time on, they sat with us in church. Eventually Brother Ritter quit the cigarettes and alcohol, and before long they both had callings in the ward.

Chapter Ten

I'm not sure what the connection is between having a bathroom that works and fertility, but within the month Charly became pregnant. With the rush of building, we had even forgotten to watch the calendar for fertile days. It had all happened without our planning.

The verdict was evident as she came bouncing out of the doctor's examining room. "I'm pregnant!" she happily announced to the entire waiting room. Then she came over to me, sat on my lap, and kissed me. The lady next to us warmly congratulated us.

"Thank you, Doctor, " she bubbled as we paid our bill and left.

"Wait a minute," I complained. "I'm the one you should thank."

Our euphoria was short-lived, however. Within a few weeks she had morning sickness, an optimistic phrase meaning in reality that she couldn't hold down anything during the morning, afternoon, or evening hours.

And how did I comfort her, you ask.

"It's all in your head," I advised, watching her lean over our lovely toilet.

She retched once more.

"I mean it, Charly. It's psychosomatic."

She stood up, stumbled to the wash basin, and washed out her mouth.

"You ever been pregnant before?"

"No."

"Then be quiet. Okay?"

Then she lurched back into the bedroom.

Naturally I felt bad.

"Don't worry about supper. I'll just eat in town before I come home from work."

She moaned something that, fortunately, I didn't hear.

But even all bad things come to an end. By the end of her fourth month, the hormone factory switched gears, and she became all at once large, alert, and full of energy. And I'm not sure why, but in spite of her bulging tummy, or maybe because of it, she became to me more beautiful than ever before.

Finally she could go back to Relief Society once more. After her experience with Sister Ritter, she came to really enjoy searching out the sisters who needed encouragement and spending time with them. And she certainly livened up the lessons.

"Sam, I've got a confession to make."

"Yeah? What?"

"I should tell you before anybody else does."

"Okay."

"In Relief Society today, the teacher asked us to share some of the things we do with our husbands that bring us closer. She made a little list on the blackboard. One sister said gardening, and Sister Pearson wrote it down. Another said bowling, and she wrote it down. After about five minutes, she had a wonderful list."

"You didn't, did you?"

"I did—I raised my hand and told them, 'My husband and I like to make love.' Poor Sister Pearson, she dropped her chalk."

It was about that time that our bishop made an appointment to speak to us. First he talked to me in his office about a calling he had in mind for Charly. My response was, "You've got to be kidding."

"You wouldn't mind if I talked to her about it, would you?"

I waited in the hall for her. When she came out, she was either laughing or crying—maybe both.

"He called me to be a counselor in the Relief Society presidency."

"I know. What did you say?"

"The man's crazy, you know. I said I didn't quilt. And he said it didn't matter. Then I told him that I don't make my own bread—he said it wasn't necessary. Then I admitted that I don't can vegetables or make your shirts—and I told him what a rotten cook I was, that to me, butter is a spice. And he just smiled and said that it was okay. So I asked him why on earth he would call me to the position. And he said, 'Because you make people feel loved and important—that's more important than quilts.'"

I held her in my arms. After a few minutes she looked at me and asked, "Do you know why I'm crying? Our bishop is the Lord's mouthpiece. This call means that Heavenly Father can use me in his church. I belong here, Sam."

We both may have shed a few tears that day—but I hid it better than she did.

* * * * *

With Charly in the Relief Society presidency, we entered our "Lamanite phase." There were nearly one hundred Sioux Indians, or Lamanites, in the area who were members of the Church, and part of her assignment in the presidency was to try to help activate them. Since the bishopric considered it unsafe for women to travel alone to some of the neighborhoods, I was recruited into the Relief Society as a visiting teaching companion to my wife. (Actually, we combined home teaching with it.)

"We're from the Mormon church," Charly said to an elderly Indian lady at one of our first doors. "May we come in?"

The woman, Sister White Horse, let us in and then mysteriously disappeared into another room. Thinking she'd be back in a minute, we sat down opposite four huge, young, apparently militant Indian men. They all had long braided hair. On the wall were several anti-white posters.

"Well," I said brightly, "it's sure cold out today, isn't it."

They looked at us but didn't say a word, or even nod their heads.

"With the wind blowing so much, it really adds to the windchill factor."

One of them took out a knife and began to cut his fingernails.

"Of course, in a few months," I continued, feeling my voice becoming more tense and higher in pitch, "when it's hot, we'll wish it were cold again. Isn't that right?" I smiled an idiotic smile.

Absolute silence.

"So I guess we'd better take advantage of the cold while we've got it. Isn't that right?"

They just stared at me. What was worse, now Charly was looking at me exactly the same way they were.

"Sam?"

"Yes."

"Be quiet."

We sat in silence for maybe five more minutes. It was unbearable to me.

Finally Sister White Horse came back to see us.

"We came to invite you to Relief Society," Charly said warmly. "It's on Tuesday at ten o'clock. I can pick you up if you like."

"Oh, yes," Sister White Horse smiled.

Then we left.

"The work with the Lamanites isn't so tough," she confidently announced as we drove home. But on Tuesday when she went to pick them up, none of the sisters she had invited went with her.

After a month of disappointment she finally said, "I know why they don't come. It's because they don't feel comfortable. Why should they? I haven't always felt comfortable there either. Not until I got to know the sisters."

That's why she helped start a Lamanite Relief Society in Sister White Horse's house in the Indian section of town. Most of the time, Charly was the only white person there. They talked mostly in Sioux, which meant that she became the shy, quiet, reserved one among them, but she tried gamely to learn their language and customs.

By the end of her seventh month of pregnancy, there were eight Lamanite sisters coming out to church.

At first we labored with the Lamanites because we felt we had so much to offer them—but as time progressed, we realized that they had much to give us. We needed them as much as they needed us. For instance:

Sister White Horse had a married daughter Charly's age whose name was Celia; her husband's name was John. They had a little six-month-old baby named Billy, a chubby, delightful boy with plenty of dark hair.

Celia was one of the sisters who nearly always attended

Relief Society. In time Charly and Celia became special friends, more like sisters, really. They did their shopping together. Celia showed Charly how to shop garage sales. Most of the things we bought for our expected baby were from garage sales. At first I was sensitive about that, but Charly assured me that she shopped only in the richest neighborhoods in town. That helped a little.

One time when we had just bought half a gallon of ice cream for dessert, on the way home, Charly suggested we stop by and share it with John and Celia. She could do things like that. Anyway, we were sitting in the living room of their small apartment. Hanging on the wall was a beautiful decoration known as a god's eye. It was made of orange and red yarn woven back and forth to make a six-sided pattern.

"That really is nice," I said in admiration.

John stood up, took it off the wall and handed it to me, and then sat down again.

"Now it's yours," Celia said.

"Oh, no, please, I wouldn't feel right about taking it."

"Please take it," she encouraged us.

I was about to object further when Charly said, "Thank you so much. It's beautiful. We'll cherish it always."

We left them with a bare wall. They had given us the one thing of beauty in their room. You tell me how many white men would do that.

That's what I meant about us needing them.

Chapter Eleven

The labor room of a hospital is no place for a man to be because it makes him feel guilty for putting a woman through all that moaning and crying.

"Ohhh!" Charly grimaced with pain. Drops of perspiration dotted her forehead.

"Now, you're not relaxing like I told you to," the nurse advised.

"How on earth is she supposed to relax?" I asked.

"She knows how—the doctor should've given her a pamphlet to read."

We had been there since one o'clock that morning, and it was now three.

The metric system has arrived in childbirth, where dilation is measured in centimeters. "Four and a half centimeters," the nurse announced as she measured.

"Is that good?" I asked.

"It's getting there," she said routinely, leaving us alone again, partitioned off by curtains from the other suffering women.

A girl moaned sharply in the bed next to where we were, but there was nobody by her side to comfort her. I peeked through the curtain separating the beds. She didn't look to be more than eighteen, and she was scared.

Charly groaned again and squeezed my hand in pain. "I've been thinking, Sam. I'm not sure if I want to go through with this or not."

I wiped her forehead. "I think it's a little late now."

"Could I have a priesthood blessing?" she asked.

I had just started to put my hands on Charly's head when the nurse came back.

"What are you doing?" she asked.

"I'm going to say a prayer with my wife."

"Oh, I'm sorry. I'll leave you alone."

I put my hands on her head and gave her a priesthood blessing. When I was finished, I kissed her lightly and told her how much I loved her.

"Hey," the girl next to us called, "could you say a prayer for me too?"

"Go ahead, Sam. I'll be all right."

I walked over to the girl's bed. "My wife and I are Mormons and the prayer I offered is what Mormons do. Is that all right?"

"It sounded so nice," the girl said.

Then I gave her a priesthood blessing. "Thank you," she said when it was over. "It was nice. Now you'd better get back to your wife."

Before long, all sorts of commotion broke out. The next time the nurse came around to check Charly, she realized she was in the last stages of labor. Suddenly the nurse was paging the doctor and Charly was being wheeled into the delivery room.

They let me put on a robe and go in to watch. The room was all lights and a table and stirrups and electronics.

"One more push!" the doctor encouraged.

And then it was out, the ugliest baby boy I had ever seen. (Nobody had warned me what it would look like before it was washed up.)

"How is he?" Charly asked as she was being wheeled away.

"Fine," I answered evasively.

"The nurse told me he looks just like you."

We called him Adam and he was born at four-fifteen in the morning. By the time I had phoned our parents from the hospital, it was five o'clock. I drove home and went to bed until noon.

When I visited Charly in the hospital that afternoon, she looked rested and happy and sore. While I was there, they brought Adam in to us. He looked so small, I was afraid I'd drop him, but she made sure I held him.

"Say something to your son," she beamed.

"Hello, this is your father speaking," I said.

"How warm, how tender," Charly teased.

Charly's roommate was the girl who had asked for a

blessing. Her name was Sheri Wilson; her husband was a rodeo clown. The rodeo had played in Rapid City a few days before. Sheri had gone on the tour with him because she wasn't due for another four weeks, but unexpectedly the pains had begun, and he had left her in their motel until he could get back from his next engagement in Montana.

"Why don't you come and stay with us until he gets back?" Charly offered.

One sore woman and a baby is one thing, but two in a house is unbelievable. For the next day or two after Charly was released from the hospital, I began to feel that my only functions in life were to run to the store for disposable diapers, to serve meals to two straggly-haired, housecoated ladies, who talked nonstop about their pains and their babies, and to listen to two healthy, crying babies.

I moved my sleeping bag into the living room and used two pillows, one to lie on and the other to put over my head to drown out the noise, which continued twenty-four hours a day.

My salvation came in an airplane from Salt Lake City, when Charly's mother showed up to help out. I picked her up at the airport and told her that mothers and children were doing well, which required an explanation about our rodeo clown's wife.

"You've got to be kidding," she said.

The cure-all for infirmity of any kind as far as Charly's mother was concerned was clam chowder; therefore, the minute her feet touched the kitchen floor, she was cooking.

During the time Sheri was with us, she asked several questions about what Mormons believed in. It was an energizer for Charly to be able to talk about the gospel with her.

After five days, her husband, a tall, lean, quiet cowboy, arrived in his dusty pickup to take his wife to stay with his folks in Wyoming until she could travel the circuit with him again.

"He's a rodeo clown?" Charly's mother asked as we watched them leave.

"Yes, why?"

"He doesn't look that funny to me."

* * * * *

Charly's mother stayed with us for a month. Without

her, we'd have been in real trouble. We found out that nursing a baby is a full-time job, and it left Charly no time to do anything else but sleep during the three hours between feedings.

But after a month I was ready for Mom to leave—the reason being that she loved Charly and Adam as much as I did. And loving them, she wanted to do things for them, like buying us a color TV, paying to have Adam's bedroom carpeted, and buying many of his clothes.

It made me furious. I guess I still remembered Mark. He was the silent visitor whenever Mom and I talked. By that time he had already achieved national prominence as a congressional candidate. We had seen him being interviewed in his race against a crusty old incumbent. Beside him was his plastic-coated, media-perfect wife. She looked like a life-sized clone of a Barbi doll. We were told that Mark was someone to keep our eyes on. I wondered if Charly had any regrets, and was sure that her mother did.

A few days later, I gently approached the subject.

"Mom, I guess you'll be leaving us soon, won't you."

"I don't know. Will I?"

"Yes, I know you need to get back to Salt Lake, but I want you and Dad to know that you're always welcome if you'd ever like to drop in some weekend."

"I appreciate that."

"Oh, not at all. Oh, when you go, you might as well take the coffee and whiskey with you. I'm sure we won't be needing them until your next visit—next year." Subtlety is one of my strong suits.

She was gone within forty-eight hours.

* * * * *

There was an interesting sacrament meeting in our ward a few months after Adam was born. The bishop, concerned about the increasing number of excommunications, spoke in behalf of fidelity.

"It's not hard to see why someone would think of an affair as being glamorous. After all, she leaves behind her the burdens of housekeeping and children and meets him when she looks beautiful and refreshed. He spends more money on her than he's spent on his wife for years. They meet in some secluded spot where they don't have to face crying children or the burdens of married life." He then went on to encourage couples to continue to court each other, to date each other weekly, and to never treat the marriage relationship as drab. He closed with an interesting idea: "Brethren, if you must spend money on a woman, spend it on your wife. If you must have an affair, have it with your own wife."

An interesting concept—one that Charly and I could enlarge upon.

"Hi there. Mind if I sit down?" I said to Charly, meeting her at a cozy restaurant where I had dropped her off five minutes earlier.

Shrugging her shoulders and treating me as a complete stranger, she said, "I guess not."

I sat across from her in the corner booth. She appeared to be uninterested as she busily studied the menu.

"You come here often?" I asked.

"No, but since the divorce, I've just had to get away once in a while."

"Oh, you're divorced," I said, my mouth drooping with pity as I reached out to hold her hand. "You poor dear."

"Yes," she sighed.

"I'll bet he was a terrible man," I said, full of understanding.

"A beast," she confided.

"I'm recently widowed," I beamed.

"Oh, I'm sorry. How recent?"

I looked at my watch. "Very recent."

The rule of our game was that we must never laugh. If I could make her laugh, then she had to empty the garbage for a week. If she made me laugh, I had to clean Adam's diaper, when I was home from work, for a week.

"That recent?" she asked, a slight smile creeping forth.

"Well, to tell you the truth, the funeral was today. I was driving back from the burial and saw this place, and thought I'd drop in. My wife hated this place and would never have come here with me. So I thought, 'Aw, what the heck. I can come here all I want now.' Right?"

Then the waitress brought our food. For a few minutes while we ate my only tactic was an obvious wink every time she looked up from her plate. I could see she was nearly ready to laugh.

"Hey, Bucko," she finally asked, "you got some kind of eye-muscle disease?"

The word *Bucko* caught me off guard and I laughed, but then quickly covered it up with a cough.

"You laughed!" she cried.

"No, it was a cough!" I denied, picturing the green mess that we were finding in Adam's diapers lately, and willing to bear false witness to avoid touching it. Charly turned to our waitress and got her to agree it was a laugh. I was sunk by the word *Bucko*.

A little more fantasy chitchat, a mock proposition, and we headed home to pay the baby-sitter, clean out the messy diapers left in our absence (I maintained that I was not responsible for them), and allow Charly enough time to nurse and burp Adam again, giving me time enough to put on a little more molding around one of our rooms (the house was nearly finished by then)—and after all that domestic routine, the fantasy could begin again.

The good part about this mock affair was that it was fun, it strengthened our love for each other, it insured that neither of us would need to have an actual affair, and it kept us intrigued with each other.

The bad part for me is that now, after Charly is gone, I can never approach another woman in a dating situation without being overwhelmingly haunted by Charly's memory.

How I wish I had never talked about being widowed.

* * * * *

One morning in September the bishop called to tell us that during the night Celia's little boy had died of pneumonia in the hospital, where he had been taken the previous night. We went right over, dropping Adam off with Louise Atkins, the other counselor in the Relief Society presidency. Louise had a young baby herself, even younger than three-month-old Adam, but she seemed to be able to handle any extra demands on her energy as a welcome addition to her life. Except for the times when she had to go back to Louise's to nurse Adam, Charly stayed with Celia and her husband all day and helped them with the arrangements.

The funeral was two days later. It was a shock as we entered the chapel to see the tiny white casket with little Billy in it. The bishop spoke about the ancestors who had welcomed Billy back into the spirit world after he died; he promised us that Billy would be exalted in the highest of God's kingdoms.

After the benediction, Celia went to the casket, took her little baby, and held him and rocked him in her arms for the last time, tears streaming down her cheeks. The aunts and grandmothers, old and tired women with the mark of pain and sorrow and disappointment etched in their faces, gathered around her and touched her and whispered in their language words of love and comfort. Finally Celia wrapped her son in a white beaded deerskin blanket and lovingly laid him back in the coffin. The staff from the mortuary efficiently supervised the removal of the body to the hearse.

After the graveside service, everyone returned to the cultural hall for a luncheon prepared by the Relief Society. When most of them had finished with their food, Celia went before them. On several tables were nearly all the earthly belongings of John and Celia. In addition, her mother, Sister White Horse, had donated several quilts and shawls for this.

One by one, each of the friends and relatives came to Celia and received from her a gift: a shawl, a quilt, beaded moccasins, a crib that had belonged to Billy. When those were gone, John gave away everything else—a chair, a TV set, their bed, their blankets. They gave away absolutely everything they owned.

"Why are they doing this?" I asked in dismay.

"It's the Indian way," was all Sister White Horse told me.

A couple of days later, Charly and I dropped by their apartment. It was bare.

Chapter Twelve

Fall in South Dakota lasts, at most, two days. One day the leaves are green and the days are warm; a day later a cold front moves down from Canada to turn the leaves yellow. The next day the stiff winds scatter the leaves on the ground and it snows.

There is a melancholy to the Dakota wind, as if the sorrow and mourning of ancient Indian ancestors had been locked up with the wind for centuries. The Dakota wind reminds us how little we affect the earth during our lives. How quickly it wipes away the memorials of the past, whether they be the decaying homesteads of forgotten settlers or the burial grounds of unnumbered native Americans.

In the first part of November Charly and I were depressed by the weather, by the promise of winter, and by the burden of sharing Celia's grief.

"Let's have a party," Charly suggested one day.

"Who would we invite?"

"Oh, just a few friends from church. Maybe some non-members so we can chalk it up to missionary work."

"Why not? I can show off our house."

The party became Charly's hobby, and before I knew what hit me, she had spent one hundred dollars. But it was some party!

The house was crammed with people—many of whom I had never met. There was a boy who carried Charly's groceries out to the car each week, and the man who serviced our water softener, and our Avon lady, and a minister from another faith who had stopped by one day to invite us to his services, and our neighbors, with the word *neighbor* defined as anyone living on the road we lived on.

The one rule for the invited members of the Church, stated plainly on the invitations, was that anyone caught talking about the Church or about babies and children would be required to wash all the dishes afterwards.

For entertainment, we had Charles Fast Bear do an Indian dance, followed by a local barbershop quartet, followed by the hit of the evening: "Now, I'd like to introduce Yvonne Williams from Kaiser Dance Studio, who has graciously consented to demonstrate belly dancing."

Miss Williams was indeed competent in her area of specialization. I held my breath, waiting for the stake president to either stop Miss Williams or else hold a court for Charly and me.

But Miss Williams got a standing ovation.

What was even more interesting was Charly's parting shot. "Now for any of you women who would like to learn more about this historic dance form, I've asked Miss Williams to come to Relief Society next Tuesday to give a few basic lessons."

The Relief Society president turned three shades of red.

"This will be after the Mother Education lesson," Charly announced.

I'm told that Tuesday was the highest attendance in Relief Society that's ever been recorded in that ward.

Near the end of the evening, one of our nonmember friends turned to our bishop and said, "You know, this has been marvelous. You Mormons really know how to have fun. Look at us all. We've all had a wonderful time, yet there's been no alcohol. I like that. Tell me, Bishop, is there some way my family could learn about your church? What do you people believe in that makes you so happy? Could you take a few minutes tonight and tell us something about your church?"

Everyone's eyes fell on the bishop, wondering if he would be the one to do the dishes that night. The table was stacked with plates caked with dried sauce.

"Some other time I'd be happy to tell you, but it's getting late now."

"Oh, it's not that late," another nonmember chirped in. "How about the rest of you? Wouldn't you all like the bishop to tell us about his church?"

Everyone enthusiastically agreed that right then there was nothing they'd rather do than hear the bishop explain about the Church.

I began to smell a rat.

"But it's so late," the bishop pleaded.

"I'm not at all tired."

The poor man stalled, made excuses, but finally broke down and started to tell them about the gospel. At first there were smiles, but when he told them about the first vision, it was quiet.

After he finished, Charly draped a dish towel around his shoulder.

Of course Charly had informed the nonmembers of her plot to get the bishop to do the dishes, and they agreed to help out by asking eagerly about the Church. *What a dirty trick to play on the bishop,* I thought as I sat and watched him do the dishes after the party. Even his wife had left him, getting a ride home with friends. "I'm not the one who talked," she said.

"Bishop, when you're through, just turn off the lights and shut the front door hard. Charly and I are going to bed."

We went in our bedroom and giggled behind the door as we listened to him work. Then, after about five minutes, we broke down and went in and helped him.

Poor bishop.

Except for one thing. Three of the couples really did get interested in the Church from that party, and two of them were later baptized. Even Miss Williams eventually ended up at BYU, and, I'm told, married in the temple.

Poor bishop indeed.

* * * * *

"What's this fifty-dollar check to Sister White Horse?" I asked one evening after work.

"It's for a star quilt. Want to see it?"

"We've already bought three from her. Why do we need another?"

"We'll give it to my parents for Christmas next year."

"They've already got enough to start a trading post."

"She and Celia needed some money to get to Rosebud."

I looked with discouragement at our ravaged bank balance. "We're nearly broke now—we can't afford to help every Indian who needs money."

"I couldn't tell her no."

"Why not? Send her to the bishop. That's what we pay fast offerings for."

About eleven that night, the phone rang and Charly answered it.

"Yes, we'll be there as soon as we can," I woke up enough to hear Charly say before hanging up.

"Who's that?" I sleepily asked.

"Sister White Horse and Celia ran into a deer on their way to Rosebud. They're at a truck stop near Wall."

"So? Can't John go out and get them?"

"He's in North Dakota this week. I told her we'd go out and get them and take them home."

"Why do we always have to be the ones?" I moaned.

"Because we're their friends. They'd do the same for us."

"But we'd never hit a deer."

It was midnight before we reached them. There were Sister White Horse, Celia, and a nephew about seven years old. I drove as fast as I could on the way home, hoping to get at least a few hours' sleep before I had to go to work.

Perhaps I got going a little too fast. Halfway through one of the small towns, we were pulled over by a local policeman.

"Having a night out on the town, hey?" he said, shining his light into the car.

"What?"

"Where'd you find them?" he asked, pointing his light in Celia's face. "In a bar?"

"Their car broke down, and they called us to come and pick them up and drive them back home."

"I bet," he sneered. I felt my stomach knot up with outrage. "Did you know you were going forty miles an hour in a thirty-mile-an-hour zone?"

"I'm sorry. Give me the ticket and let's get it over with."

"Not so fast. Get out of the car, all of you. I'm going to check for opened liquor bottles."

I just looked at him.

"You heard me, get out of the car."

We all climbed out and he shone his flashlight over the floorboards and looked under the seats and in the glove compartment.

"I haven't had anything to drink," I told him.

"Okay then, all I need you to do is to walk from there to me in a straight line."

I couldn't believe this was happening.

"C'mon, Sam, you can do it," Charly encouraged.

"Of course I can do it! But why should he ask me? It's just because we've got Indians in the car."

I walked over to the cop.

"Well?"

"Not bad. May I look in your trunk?"

I opened the trunk. "Well?"

"You must've thrown it out when you saw me coming." He gave me the ticket for speeding.

"Can I go now?"

"Sure, just one thing—off the record. Why do you have the Indians in your car?"

When we got home it was one-thirty, and I could have slept the rest of the night, but I was so steamed up that I couldn't sleep much at all.

The next day after work, Charly told me that she had phoned all her high school friends who now were in business in New York and asked them to carry some Indian crafts in their stores.

"Four of them agreed!" she exclaimed proudly. "We can help Sister White Horse become more independent. Then people won't push her around so much."

"Charly, that's great!"

"Aren't you going to ask me how much the phone calls cost?"

I paused. "How many friends did you have in high school that are now in business?"

"Twenty-three," she said demurely.

* * * * *

"Sam?" Charly asked on the phone one Tuesday near the end of November, "can you come over to church? There's a man asking for a handout, and we're in the middle of Relief Society. We need the priesthood here."

I told one of the other programmers that I'd be out for a while and then I drove to the church.

The man, an Indian, had been drinking. As far as I could tell he wanted money for transportation to get him to California. All I could tell him was that he would have to talk to the bishop, but when we tried to phone the bishop, his secretary told us that he was out of town for the day. The man, whose name was Reuben Kills First, didn't want to go anywhere, and until I could figure out a way to get him out of the building, I had to remain to watch him.

He rambled on about various subjects as we sat in the hall; occasionally I nodded yes to something he would say, but I didn't have much interest in him or what he said.

Then he asked me a question I'll never forget. "Do you know Jesus Christ?"

The smell of liquor permeated the air around him, and I had listened to his swear words and vulgar language, and I thought, *what right does he have to ask me that?* But with what I thought was great patience, I answered, "In this church, we know more about Jesus Christ than any other church in the world."

"That's not what I want to know. Do *you* know Jesus Christ?"

I remembered the Christians I had met on my mission who used that question as a weapon against the Mormons—implying that all that was needed was one decision, and then everything else, including baptism, was unnecessary.

"We have a prophet who receives revelation from the Savior. This is the Church of Jesus Christ."

He leaned forward, and the smell of his breath disgusted me. "Do you personally know Jesus Christ?"

I was furious. How dare he, a drunk, ask me that!

"Do you know Jesus Christ?"

Along with my anger, I also felt the awareness of a great vulnerability. He drifted into other subjects. But I knew that he had found a weakness in me.

A few minutes later he let me drive him downtown; in fifteen minutes he had walked out of my life forever.

After supper that night, I took a walk in the woods and thought about how I felt about the Savior. I knew the doctrine about him. I had read the scriptures and I held the priesthood and I did my home teaching and tried to fulfill my callings. Even so, I had to conclude that I could be closer to him than I was.

That day I set a goal to review the scriptures with the idea of trying to become closer to him, to love him more fully. What were the results? No change in doctrine, no decrease in my honor of the prophet, but my love for Jesus increased and I began to see him as a man who could be reached and loved and cherished. The idea of performing a calling because of duty decreased, and I could see that a calling is an opportunity to serve the Savior.

One particular passage in my reading puzzled me—the raising of Lazarus. The Savior knew several days in advance that Lazarus was sick and that he was going to die, and that He would raise him from the dead. He understood that from the beginning. Lazarus's death at that time was to last only four days.

When Jesus met Martha and Mary after they'd buried Lazarus, they reproached him for not being there when Lazarus was sick. As they walked to the tomb where they'd laid him, the scriptures say that Jesus wept. Why? Why did he weep when he knew that Lazarus would come to life in five minutes? Why did he weep when he knew that, in a few minutes, Mary and Martha would be happier than at any other time? Why did he weep when he knew that their sorrow was only a breeding ground for their approaching joy?

Why did he weep?

* * * * *

Christmas that year was the best one for us because we had Adam. He was only six months old and wasn't even walking yet, but he smiled. I would go to any lengths to get him to smile, and Charly said she only hoped nobody watched me as I made faces to make him laugh.

I had received a Christmas bonus from the company and used it selfishly for the thing that would give me the most joy. I bought presents for Adam: a baseball glove, an electric train, a giant Panda bear stuffed doll, ten little books with pictures of animals, and a wind-up musical Ferris wheel.

"Who did you get the train for?" Charly asked on

Christmas Eve as I played train after setting it up around our Christmas tree.

It was a wonderful Christmas.

* * * * *

"Sam, I'd like to get away with you on a little trip," Charly purred in my ear one night in March.

"Oh yeah?" I asked, perking up. "Where would you like to go?"

"Does it matter to you?"

"No, I guess not, as long as we're alone."

"Wonderful," she said, heading for the phone.

"Who are you calling?"

"Sister White Horse. To tell her we can take her to the reservation in Pine Ridge on Friday night."

"Sister White Horse? How did she get into this conversation?"

"She's got sores all over her hands so she can't do any beadwork. The doctors at the Indian Health Center have been giving her medicine for three months but it hasn't done much good. She wants to visit the medicine man."

"C'mon, Charly, you're not serious. You don't believe all that mumbo jumbo, do you?"

"Not me, but she does, and she needs a ride to Pine Ridge. We can stay at some romantic hideaway Friday night and then give her a ride back home on Saturday morning. Louise says she'll take Adam overnight."

"What about nursing him?" I asked, hoping to find a flaw in the plan.

"Louise can nurse him along with her baby."

"You mean both of them? She'll do that?"

"Oh sure, she says she has plenty of milk."

By then, Charly was talking to Sister White Horse on the phone and I knew I'd been outflanked again.

After work on Friday we dropped Adam off with Louise and then picked up Sister White Horse. Those two talked and giggled like school kids all the way to the reservation. People who say Indians are quiet and reserved don't know them very well.

One of the stories Sister White Horse told was about an

old Indian man who was losing his eyesight. He couldn't see much anymore, and one night he dreamed a dream, and the next day he had his two grandsons walk him around until they found a skunk. He got down on his hands and knees in front of the skunk; the skunk willingly sprayed him in the eyes. And then he could see.

That became the Indian way. I pictured old men and women stumbling around in the forest trying to find a skunk to spray them. Then one night a medicine man dreamed that he could kill the skunk, cut him open, and use the pouch of spray for the eyes.

When we reached Pine Ridge, it was seven-thirty at night. I was all set to drop Sister White Horse off and then head for a motel with Charly.

"Where does the medicine man live?" I asked.

"Just over the hill, I think," she said vaguely.

We drove for half an hour.

"How much farther?"

"Just a little."

Another half hour went by. We switched from a paved road to a graveled road to a dirt road to two well-worn ruts to a faint mark where only a few cars had ever been before.

Finally we pulled up to a small, one-room shack in the middle of nowhere. It was dark outside; the only light for miles was a small glow from a kerosene lamp in the shack.

"Come in and meet him," Sister White Horse asked us.

No thanks, I thought. "Okay," Charly answered eagerly.

Charles Blue Thunder looked like a medicine man. He was old and his face looked as if it had been sculpted by an artist who liked deep crevices. It had been carved by at least sixty years of being in the Dakota wind. Even so, in his little shack, there was a nobility about him.

He examined Sister White Horse's hands, then went to a shelf and gave her a canning jar of cloudy water. He told her in Dakota language, she told us later, to wash her hands with the water twice a day and to pray each day and to walk outside early in the morning before the sun was up. I wasn't impressed.

"What's in the jars?" I asked.

"Roots from Canada. I boil them and then grind them up. They come from a lake there."

"How did you come across this cure?"

"In my dreams," he said.

You bet, I thought. "Well, Charly, we'd better get back to town now."

"No, stay," Charles pleaded. "My daughter has made food."

"We really can't," I said, anxious to find a motel.

But Charly was entranced with him.

"Sam, we really haven't had supper yet."

We ate soup made from corn and potatoes and jerky and wild turnips. While we ate, he told Charly how to find wild turnips. For dessert we had fry bread and wojape, an Indian pudding.

"You like it," he said, smiling as I finished my third piece of fry bread.

"Yes, very much."

Sister White Horse laughed at the sight of me eating so eagerly. "We Indians really know how to cook. We could make a lot of money showing the whites our recipes, but we keep our cooking to ourselves."

I yawned. It was now nine-thirty. "Well, now we really have to go. Sister White Horse, we'll pick you up in the morning."

"You stay here tonight," Charles offered.

"Oh no," I objected, set on being alone with Charly for one whole night without Adam disturbing us.

"Sam, how are we going to find our way back to Pine Ridge in the dark?"

"We'll manage," I bluffed.

"And if we do, how will we ever make it back out here tomorrow morning?"

I remembered all the turns we had made to get here. She had me again. Sadly I shrugged my shoulders.

"We'll stay," Charly told the others.

Half an hour later I wrapped a blanket around myself and lay down on the floor beside Charly, who was next to Sister White Horse, who was next to Charles, who was next to his fifty-year-old daughter, who was next to three dogs.

"Sam," Charly whispered in my ear, "I'm definitely going to make this up to you."

The facts are that Sister White Horse's hands cleared up within two weeks. When the visiting nurse saw the sudden improvement, she told the doctor, and within a day he sent a message to her.

"He wants to know what's in the medicine," Sister

White Horse grinned, "but we're not giving it to any white man."

"Good for you," I caught myself saying.

Chapter Thirteen

It began in April with complaints of pain in her side, but we blamed it on her having to pick up Adam all the time. But the pains became worse, and I finally persuaded her to see a doctor. Over a period of two weeks, he ran a series of tests. Then he asked me to come in and talk to him.

At first he asked about Adam and me, where my parents lived. I knew something was wrong because he was small-talking with me when he had a waiting room full of patients thumbing through *Good Housekeeping*.

"What's wrong with my wife?"

He studied me closely and then said simply, "Cancer. It's all through her body. I'm afraid there isn't much we can do now."

"No, you're wrong," I exploded. "If you're such a great doctor, what are you doing in this town? I'm going to find a doctor who knows what he's doing!"

I hurried home to her; she was resting on the couch.

"Charly, you owe me a night alone. Right?"

"Right."

"Fine. Does it matter where we go?"

"Why?"

"I have a sudden wild urge to spend the night with you in Rochester, Minnesota," I replied, picking up the phone to make plane reservations.

"That's where the Mayo Clinic is, isn't it?"

"Oh, really?" I lied. "Well, while we're there we might as well drop in and have them take a look at you."

"Sam, don't. I don't want to go anywhere."

I stopped dialing. "What do you want to do?"

"Stay here in my home with my baby and my husband for as long as I can."

I hung up and wondered what she knew.

"I phoned the nurse this afternoon and impersonated my mother. They told me what's wrong."

"They don't know anything. We can move you to Rochester or Denver or Salt Lake City. We could all move there until you're better."

"No, I want to be here watching my son grow up in his home."

I built a little enclosed patio in our backyard and assembled a baby swing set for Adam. Charly wanted a flower garden, so I picked up some plants in May and stuck them into the ground.

Even as short as the growing season is in South Dakota, they lasted longer than she did.

One night about eight o'clock, Louise Atkins was at our door.

"Charly said this morning she wasn't feeling well. I thought maybe she'd like me to nurse Adam." When she went in to Charly and asked her, Charly started to cry with relief. "Oh, thank you. I was worrying about that so much."

"No problem," Louise said quickly.

Nothing was ever a problem for Louise. She continued to nurse Adam twice a day for the next month. Often, when she came, she would have a big pot of stew. "Can you help me out? I didn't know I had so much when I made this, and Rick refuses to eat it more than one meal, so if you don't take it, I'll just have to throw it out."

We always helped Louise out by taking the food she had cooked too much of, or by having Adam help use up some of her milk supply, or by allowing the Relief Society sisters, who absolutely needed a service project and couldn't think of a thing to do, to come in and clean for us.

In the beginning, while I was still working, I would come home from work and there would be a casserole in the oven, fresh homemade bread on the counter, a salad and Jello in the refrigerator. Most of the time I never knew who had brought them. And somehow during my time at work, the laundry was mysteriously done, the carpet vacuumed, the diapers washed and folded. To this day I don't know who did it.

The Relief Society is like that.

Both sets of parents came as soon as they heard. It was very difficult. We couldn't seem to face it head-on all the time, even though we all knew what was coming. We found ourselves fantasizing about new treatments, about places in Mexico where they cured all diseases with natural herbs, about people who had suddenly gotten well from the same disease. And we never mentioned, even to each other, the word *cancer*.

My father and I administered to her. We wanted to promise her that she would completely recover, but there was a feeling that it was not to be. We ended up promising her that God loved her and Adam and me, and that he would provide for all our needs.

*　*　*　*　*

Charly wanted to stay at home as long as she could, and so in May I quit my job. Then I was forced to ask our parents for help, the one thing that had always been the hardest for me. But suddenly I was dependent upon everyone. Our parents jointly set up what they called a "bottomless checking account," and they made sure I never got the bank statement. I just wrote checks from it.

"Sam, quit hovering over me—I hate it when you hover."

This was a good day. Near the last, every other day was good.

I sat down on the bed beside her. "It's time for a pill now."

"I don't want it yet. It fogs my mind and I want to talk."

We had avoided talking about her condition for days and were back to talking about the weather again, just as we had on our first date. So I wasn't prepared for what she said.

"Sam, where are you going to find another wife after I'm gone?"

"I've got a wife. We were married for time and eternity. You'll always be my wife."

"I mean a wife who can give you what you need."

"I don't need anything, Charly."

"C'mon, you're not even thirty years old yet. Of course

you're going to need a wife. And my son needs a mother. So where will you go?"

"I don't want to talk about it."

"But I do. I've thought about the single women around here and there's none of them in the Church you'd be happy with, is there?"

I started to cry. "I don't want anyone else. I want you."

"C'mon, Sam, where's your male chauvinism when you really need it?"

I was kneeling by the bed with my head next to her and I was crying. She reached out and touched my hair. "It's going to be all right," she assured me.

"No, it isn't."

"I've thought about it and I've prayed about it," she said, running her fingers over my hair. "When Jesus was about to die, he told the apostles that there were many mansions in heaven and that he was going to prepare a place for them. And that's what I'm going to do, Sam. I'll go ahead and find us a nice little mansion. Sam, look at me."

I looked up and tried to memorize every feature of her face.

"In fifty years you come and meet me in our little mansion—okay?"

"Okay," I said.

"Do you want a swimming pool, or is that too ostentatious?"

"Charly, I can't take this."

"Poor Sam," she said as my tears cascaded down. "Answer me about the swimming pool. Do you want it or not?"

"No."

"Me either. They're just a lot of bother. But a racquetball court—you'd like that, wouldn't you?"

"Yes."

I sat beside her and held her hand. Somehow making definite plans about our being together after this life took away some of the terror.

"Now, about your next wife, Sam. I suggest you move back to Salt Lake and move in with your parents. That way Adam's grandmas can spoil him rotten. Then you look around for someone. Now, this is important, and I want you to remember it. Find someone I can get along with. You're not only looking for a wife for you, but you're looking for a

92

sister for me. I understand I'll have to share you with her in heaven, and we don't want any violent arguments between me and her there, do we? What would the neighbors think? Especially if the neighbors are people like Moses or Harold B. Lee."

"I'll remember."

"Oh," she said with a grin, "and it'd be all right with me if she loves to do housework and cook."

* * * * *

That was a good day, but there were bad days.

Adam was almost a year old, a handsome boy with eyes like large black olives. He had few words—the ones he needed the most: "dink" for "drink," for example. Charly could occasionally get him to say "Daddy." But he didn't seem to feel any great motivation to talk.

At first I didn't realize what she was doing. I only knew that when she was awake and feeling good enough, she went with him through each of the children's books with the pictures of animals.

"Bird, Adam. Bird."

He would look at the picture and mumble something.

"No, honey, it's a bird. Can you say it for me?"

Then I would leave to go downstairs to wash up some diapers, and when I came up she'd be looking at another book with him.

One afternoon as I was in the kitchen peeling some potatoes, I heard her again.

"Mommy, Adam, Mommy."

No answer.

"Mommy, Adam, please say it. Mommy."

I peeked into the living room where she was sitting. She had a picture of herself and was pointing to the picture, and then to herself, and was saying over and over again, "Mommy, Adam, Mommy."

I ducked back into the kitchen and cried silently while she attempted to leave in his mind some record of her presence.

"Please, baby, please say my name. I'm your mommy. Please remember me."

But Adam crawled off, and then she broke down too.

* * * * *

A few days later I woke up at two o'clock as I had been doing automatically for the past weeks to give her a pill. I turned on a night light so I could see to make it into the kitchen for a glass of water. Charly wasn't in bed.

I found her in Adam's room by his crib, her arms stretched through the bars of the crib, touching him, sobbing quietly. Apparently she had crawled into his room, wanting to hold him again. But because of her weakness she couldn't lift him, and had sunk to the floor in defeat. She could only reach him through the bars of the crib.

I knelt down beside her.

"I want my baby," she cried.

She wouldn't leave him at night after that. I dragged in the top mattress from our bed and plopped it on the floor beside Adam's crib and then brought in the blankets and pillows. We slept that way for the rest of the time she was still in the house. Adam would first go to sleep in his crib, then I would lift him out and place him between us on the mattress on the floor.

Chapter Fourteen

I felt great heartache as I watched Charly slowly become weaker, but even so, after we had talked about continuing our marriage in heaven, I felt that our love would never die.

I wanted to know how this appeared to the Savior. He lives and knows each of us by name, and his love for us is completely unconditional. How did he view the imminent passing away of my wife? We had been faithful to the covenants we made in the temple. The Savior was aware of the joy awaiting in heaven after the resurrection. This thing that to us was such a great tragedy, what was it to him, who saw beyond the grave? Did he understand the depths of my sorrow?

Then I remembered the raising of Lazarus—Mary and Martha weeping for the loss of their dear brother as they all trudged up the hill to the tomb. Jesus was certain that in five minutes Lazarus would come forth. What if he had turned to Mary and told her not to cry and that everything would be okay? What if he had treated lightly her sorrow?

Instead, he wept.

He wept because they wept and because he shared their sorrow. He wept because he loved them, and whatever grief they carried, even for a short time, he shared it with them.

He would not leave me comfortless because he loves me, and he loves Charly, and he loves our son Adam. He wept because he loves us.

* * * * *

By the middle of August, Charly's condition had deteriorated so much that I couldn't take care of her by myself anymore. I had to get her to a hospital.

Louise came by to take care of Adam. I picked Charly up in my arms and we walked into Adam's room, where he had just been put down for a nap. Louise picked him up again so Charly could kiss him one more time.

"Mommy," he smiled, saying the word for the first time.

As we passed the shopping center, Charly looked out the window and asked me to stop. There, in the parking lot, set up for the weekend in its red, white, and blue splendor, was a Ferris wheel. I drove as close as I could to it and parked.

"Please," she asked.

Leaving her there in the car, I talked to the attendant, offering him a twenty-dollar bill if he would reserve it for us for one ride. Then I walked to the car and gingerly picked her up in my arms and held her while we soared again over the uncaring crowds below.

After two or three minutes the pain was too intense, and she begged me to take her to the hospital.

When she was in the hospital, I divided my time between her and Adam. My son and I spent hours in the park. For some reason I hated to go home.

At the last she was kept heavily sedated. When our parents came, near the end, she didn't even recognize them.

I sat by her bed and, because of her thirst, put little drops of water one by one into her mouth. I think she appreciated it, but she never gained consciousness enough to tell me.

Then it was over.

She died on my birthday. I've never been able to decide what she meant by that. I'm going to ask her when we meet again.

Before the funeral, men from the elders quorum came with a rental truck and loaded our belongings. When my mother-in-law understood what I intended to do with them, she cautiously asked why. I told her that it was what Charly would want.

Charly would have liked the funeral, not because it was so crowded, nor for the nice things people said about her, nor because the Relief Society sisters sang two songs, but because there were so many Lamanites there. You see, they had adopted her.

There was a graveside service on that windy, blustery day, and the wind kept blowing over the flower vases while we gathered to dedicate the grave. It couldn't even wait until we left.

After the graveside service and the luncheon, I gave away everything that had been loaded in the truck. I started with the things that didn't mean anything to me—the furniture. But when it came time to give away the clothes that had been hers, it was very difficult for me. Charly's mother came and stood by my side and helped me. I'm sure some of the clothes had belonged to Charly since before she had been married; some of them must have brought back memories to her mother, but she bravely assisted me. We gave most of her clothes to Celia. I'm sure Charly approves.

I gave everything away, all that we had in our home, except what Adam and I needed in Salt Lake City, and Adam's Christmas presents, which we kept. Then I drove both sets of parents to the airport and waited with them until the plane was called.

Charly's mother, her face without make-up, threw her arms around me and cried, "Sam, there couldn't have been a better husband to her than you. She loved you so."

Her father grabbed my hand. "Please—always be our son. We don't have anyone else now."

My parents told me that as soon as they got home that day, they would arrange a place for Adam and me to stay. "I'm going to buy a swing set for the backyard right today. It'll be waiting for Adam when you arrive tomorrow."

The plane was called again, we hugged each other, and they left.

As I drove home, I passed the restaurant where Charly and I had played out our little fantasy and my words came back, "I'm recently widowed." I pulled up to the house and walked one more time through the now-empty rooms. In that house I could tell you every nail that Charly had driven.

It was all gone, and I was as empty as the rooms that now echoed my footsteps.

Just as we were about to leave the house for the last time, a beat-up old pickup rattled its way up our road. It stopped in our driveway and a young, dusty couple, both in jeans and western shirts, approached us happily. The woman was carrying a little boy in her arms.

"Do you remember us?" she asked.

"No, I'm sorry."

"I'm Sheri Wilson and this is my husband, Don. Don't you remember?"

I stared at them numbly.

"I stayed with you after I had my baby."

"Oh, yes," I answered.

"We're on our way to a Labor Day rodeo, but we just had to stop in and say hello. Is Charly here?" she asked, looking at the house.

I couldn't tell them. Maybe I wanted to spare them the sorrow, but I don't think that was it. They were the first people I should have informed that my wife was dead, and I couldn't bring myself to say it. If I never said it, maybe it wouldn't be true.

"She's not here right now," I said.

"Oh, that's too bad," Sheri said. "Look, when you see her, tell her that after she told me so much about the Mormons, Don and I looked into it. We were baptized six months ago. Tell her we're planning to go through the temple and be sealed as soon as we can. And tell her how much we love her for what she did for us."

"I'll tell her when I see her again," I said, as cheerfully as I could.

I watched their pickup bounce away from me down the dusty road.

Then Adam and I left for Salt Lake City to find a home—well, at least a temporary home—until the time when we're called Home and we find out what Charly has arranged for us that will be more permanent.